ALSO BY ROBERT AITKEN

Encouraging Words
Pantheon Books, 1994

The Practice of Perfection
Pantheon Books, 1994

The Gateless Barrier
North Point Press, 1991

The Dragon Who Never Sleeps
Larkspur Press, 1990

Taking the Path of Zen
North Point Press, 1982

A Zen Wave
Weatherhill, 1978

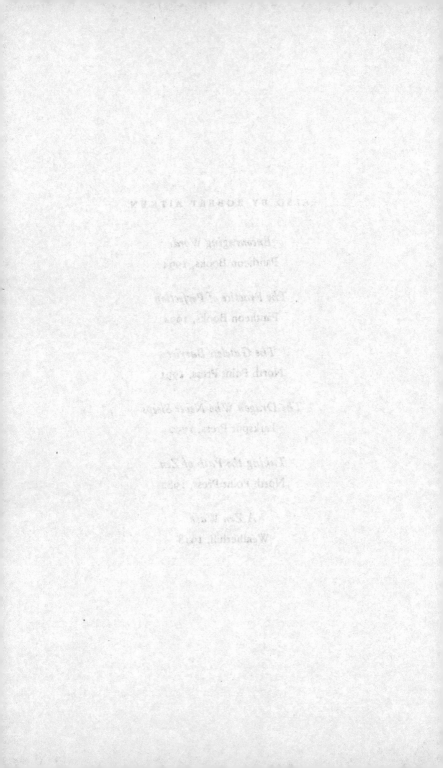

The Mind of Clover

Essays in
Zen Buddhist Ethics

Robert Aitken

North Point Press
Farrar, Straus and Giroux
New York

North Point Press
A division of Farrar, Straus and Giroux
New York
3 5 7 9 10 8 6 4 2

To my Zen master, Yamada Kōun Rōshi,
who shows me Right Action,
and to Diamond Sangha students
who help me do it.

Contents

x Contents

Acknowledgments

Most of these essays appeared in earlier forms in *Blind Donkey*, and all appeared in *Mind Moon Circle*. *Kahawai: Journal of Women and Zen* published "Not Killing," as did *Impulse*. *The Middle Way* and *Ten Directions* both published "Not Stealing." "Gandhi, Dōgen, and Deep Ecology" appeared in *Zero* and in *Simply Living*, and is anthologized in *Deep Ecology*, edited by Bill Devall and George Sesshins, Gibbs M. Smith, Inc.

Benjamin Lynn Olson transcribed the first talks I gave on the precepts in 1976, and suggested that I make them into a book. His transcriptions were very useful to me in the course of revisions I made in the talks over the years, and I am very grateful to him for his help and encouragement.

Many people have read the manuscript and made useful suggestions for revision. First and foremost among these is Wendell Berry, whose wise and incisive comments prompted me to make important changes. Stephen Mitchell marked up every essay before its publication in *Blind Donkey* and rereading the work now I can see his influence on almost every page. P. Nelson Foster edited the essays for *Blind Donkey* and helped me very much with formulating my points in logical sequence.

I must also acknowledge the assistance of Anne Aitken, Teresa Vast, Gary Snyder, Michael Kieran, John Tarrant, and others who read all or portions of the manuscript and made helpful comments. I bow to my typists as well: Sarah Bender, Victoria Chau, Diane Epstein, and Stephenie L'Heureux.

Kazuaki Tanahashi made the calligraphy "Tadashii (Upright)" for the title page of the book, and I thank him for his creative, generous gift. Finally I want to thank the staff of North Point Press: Jack Shoemaker, Tom Christensen, Dave Bullen, and the others, who turn manuscripts into books with genius and dispatch.

Acknowledgments

Most of these essays appeared in earlier forms in *Blind Donkey*, and all appeared in *Mind Moon Circle*. *Kahawai: Journal of Women and Zen* published "Not Killing," as did *Impulse*. *The Middle Way* and *Ten Directions* both published "Not Stealing." "Gandhi, Dōgen, and Deep Ecology" appeared in *Zero* and in *Simply Living*, and is anthologized in *Deep Ecology*, edited by Bill Devall and George Sesshins, Gibbs M. Smith, Inc.

Benjamin Lynn Olson transcribed the first talks I gave on the precepts in 1976, and suggested that I make them into a book. His transcriptions were very useful to me in the course of revisions I made in the talks over the years, and I am very grateful to him for his help and encouragement.

Many people have read the manuscript and made useful suggestions for revision. First and foremost among these is Wendell Berry, whose wise and incisive comments prompted me to make important changes. Stephen Mitchell marked up every essay before its publication in *Blind Donkey* and rereading the work now I can see his influence on almost every page. P. Nelson Foster edited the essays for *Blind Donkey* and helped me very much with formulating my points in logical sequence.

I must also acknowledge the assistance of Anne Aitken, Teresa Vast, Gary Snyder, Michael Kieran, John Tarrant, and others who read all or portions of the manuscript and made helpful comments. I bow to my typists as well: Sarah Bender, Victoria Chau, Diane Epstein, and Stephenie L'Heureux.

Kazuaki Tanahashi made the calligraphy "Tadashii (Upright)" for the title page of the book, and I thank him for his creative, generous gift. Finally I want to thank the staff of North Point Press: Jack Shoemaker, Tom Christensen, Dave Bullen, and the others, who turn manuscripts into books with genius and dispatch.

"I see nobody on the road," said Alice.

"I only wish I had such eyes," the King remarked in a fretful tone. "To be able to see Nobody! And at that distance too!"

Lewis Carroll
Through the Looking-Glass

Each time the wave breaks
  The raven
Gives a little jump.

Nissha
(Translated by R. H. Blyth,
Senryū: Japanese Satirical Verses)

The Mind
of Clover

CHAPTER ONE

The Nature
of the Precepts

The precepts of Zen Buddhism derive from the rules that governed the *Sangha*, or community of monks and nuns who gathered about Śākyamuni Buddha. As the religion of Buddhism developed through the Mahayana schools, the meaning of sangha broadened to include all beings, not just monks and nuns, and not just human beings. Community continues to be a treasure of the religion today, and the precepts continue to be a guide. My purpose in this book is to clarify them for Western students of Buddhism as a way to help make Buddhism a daily practice.

Without the precepts as guidelines, Zen Buddhism tends to become a hobby, made to fit the needs of the ego. Selflessness, as taught in the Zen center, conflicts with the indulgence that is encouraged by society. The student is drawn back and forth, from outside to within the Zen center, tending to use the center as a sanctuary from the difficulties experienced in the world. In my view, the true Zen Buddhist center is not a mere sanctuary, but a source from which ethically motivated people move outward to engage in the larger community.

There are different sets of precepts, depending on the

teachings of the various schools of Buddhism. In the Harada-Yasutani line of Zen, which derives from the *Sōtō* school, the "Sixteen Bodhisattva Precepts" are studied and followed. These begin with the "Three Vows of Refuge":

> I take refuge in the Buddha;
> I take refuge in the Dharma;
> I take refuge in the Sangha.

Buddha, Dharma, and Sangha can be understood here to mean realization, truth, and harmony. These Three Vows of Refuge are central to the ceremony of initiation to Buddhism in all of its schools.

The way of applying these vows in daily life is presented in "The Three Pure Precepts," which derive from a *gāthā* (didactic verse) in the *Dhammapada* and other early Buddhist books:

> Renounce all evil;
> practice all good;
> keep your mind pure—
> thus all the Buddhas taught.[1]

In Mahayana Buddhism, these lines underwent a change reflecting a shift from the ideal of personal perfection to the ideal of oneness with all beings. The last line was dropped, and the third rewritten:

> Renounce all evil;
> practice all good;
> save the many beings.

These simple moral injunctions are then explicated in detail in "The Ten Grave Precepts," "Not Killing, Not Stealing, Not Misusing Sex," and so on, which are discussed in the next ten chapters.

These sixteen Bodhisattva precepts are accepted by the Zen student in the ceremony called *Jukai* ("Receiving the Precepts"), in which the student acknowledges the guidance of the Buddha. They are studied privately with the *rōshi*, the teacher, but are not taken up in *teishō* (Dharma talks), or discussed at any length in Zen commentaries.

I think the reason for this esotericism is the fear of misunderstanding. When Bodhidharma says that in self-nature there is no thought of killing, as he does in his comment on the First Grave Precept, this was his way of saving all beings. When Dōgen Kigen Zenji says that you should forget yourself, as he does throughout his writing, this was his way of teaching openness to the mind of the universe. However, it seems that teachers worry that "no thought of killing" and "forgetting the self" could be misunderstood to mean that one has license to do anything, so long as one does it forgetfully.

I agree that the pure words of Bodhidharma and Dogen Zenji can be misunderstood, but for this very reason I think it is the responsibility of Zen teachers to interpret them correctly. Takuan Sōhō Zenji fails to live up to this responsibility, it seems to me, in his instructions to a samurai:

> The uplifted sword has no will of its own, it is all of emptiness. It is like a flash of lightning. The man who is about to be struck down is also of emptiness, as is the one who wields the sword. . . .
>
> Do not get your mind stopped with the sword you raise; forget about what you are doing, and strike the enemy. Do not keep your mind on the person before you. They are all of emptiness, but beware of your mind being caught in emptiness.[2]

The Devil quotes scripture, and *Māra*, the incarnation of ignorance, can quote the *Abhidharma*. The fallacy of the

Way of the Samurai is similar to the fallacy of the Code of the Crusader. Both distort what should be a universal view into an argument for partisan warfare. The catholic charity of the Holy See did not include people it called pagans. The vow of Takuan Zenji to save all beings did not encompass the one he called the enemy.[3]

This is very different from the celebrated koan of Nan-ch'üan killing the cat:

> The Priest Nan-ch'uan found monks of the Eastern and Western halls arguing about a cat. He held up the cat and said, "Everyone! If you can say something, I will spare this cat. If you can't say anything, I will cut off its head." No one could say anything, so Nansen cut the cat into two.[4]

Like all koans, this is a folk story, expressive of essential nature as it shows up in a particular setting. The people who object to its violence are those who refuse to read fairy tales to their children. Fairy tales have an inner teaching which children grasp intuitively, and koans are windows onto spiritual knowledge. Fairy tales do not teach people to grind up bones of Englishmen to make bread, and koans do not instruct us to go around killing pets.

Spiritual knowledge is a powerful tool. Certain teachings of Zen Buddhism and certain elements of its practice can be abstracted and used for secular purposes, some of them benign, such as achievement in sports; some nefarious, such as murder for hire. The Buddha Dharma with its integration of wisdom and compassion must be taught in its fullness. Otherwise its parts can be poison when they are misused.

"Buddha Dharma" means here "Buddhist doctrine," but "Dharma" has a broader meaning than "doctrine," and indeed it carries with it an entire culture of meaning. Misunderstanding of the precepts begins with misunderstanding of the Dharma, and likewise clear insight into the Dharma opens the way to upright practice.

First of all, the Dharma is the mind, not merely the brain, or the human spirit. "Mind" with a capital letter, if you like. It is vast and fathomless, pure and clear, altogether empty, and charged with possibilities. It is the unknown, the unnameable, from which and as which all beings come forth.

Second, these beings that come forth also are the Dharma. People are beings, and so are animals and plants, so are stones and clouds, so are postulations and images that appear in dreams. The Dharma is phenomena and the world of phenomena.

Third, the Dharma is the interaction of phenomena and the law of that interaction. "Dharma" and its translations mean "law" in all languages of Buddhist lineage, Sanskrit, Chinese, and Japanese. The Dharma is the law of the universe, a law that may be expressed simply: "One thing depends upon another." Cause leads to effect, which in turn is cause leading to effect, in an infinite, dynamic web of endless dimensions. The operation of this law is called "karma."

Many people feel there is something mechanical in the karmic interpretation of the Dharma. "Cause and effect," however dynamic, can imply something blind, so it is important to understand that "affinity" is another meaning of karma. When a man and woman in Japan meet and fall in love, commonly they will say to each other, "We must have known each other in previous lives." Western couples may not say such a thing, but they will feel this same sense of affinity. What we in the West attribute to coincidence, the Asians attribute to affinity. "Mysterious karma" is an expression you will commonly hear.

Affinity and coincidence are surface manifestations of the

organic nature of the universe, in which nothing occurs independently or from a specific set of causes, but rather everything is intimately related to everything else, and things happen by the tendencies of the whole in the context of particular circumstances. The Law of Karma expresses the fact that the entire universe is in equilibrium, as Marco Pallis has said.[5]

This intimate interconnection is found in nature by biologists and physicists today as it was once found by the Buddhist geniuses who composed Mahayana texts, particularly the *Prajñāpāramitā* (Perfection of Wisdom) and the *Huayen* (Garland of Flowers) sutras. These are compendiums of religious literature that offer important tools for understanding the Dharma, and thus understanding the precepts.

The *Heart Sutra*, which condenses the *Prajnaparamita* into just a couple of pages, begins with the words:

> *Avalokiteśvara*, doing deep prajnaparamita,
> clearly saw that all five *skandhas* are empty,
> transforming suffering and distress.[6]

Avalokiteshvara is the Bodhisattva of Mercy, who by his or her very name expresses the fact that the truth not merely sets you free, it also brings you into compassion with others. In the Far East, the name is translated in two ways, "The One Who Perceives the [Essential] Self at Rest," and "The One Who Perceives the Sounds of the World." In Japanese these names are *Kanjizai* and *Kanzeon* respectively.

Kanjizai, the one who perceives the self at rest, clearly sees that the skandhas, phenomena and our perceptions of them, are all without substance. This is the truth that liberates and transforms. Kanzeon, the one who perceives the sounds of the world in this setting of empty infinity, is totally free of self-preoccupation, and so is tuned to the suffering other creatures. Kanjizai and Kanzeon are the same Bodhisattva of Mercy.

"Bodhisattva" is a compound Sanskrit word that means "enlightenment-being." There are three implications of the term: a being who is enlightened, a being who is on the path of enlightenment, and one who enlightens beings. The whole of Mahayana metaphysics is encapsulated in this triple archetype. Avalokiteshvara is the Buddha from the beginning and also is on the path to realizing that fact. Moreover, this self-realization is not separate from the Tao ("the Way") of saving others. For you and me, this means that saving others is saving ourselves, and saving ourselves is realizing what has always been true. As disciples of Shakyamuni Buddha, we exemplify these three meanings. Senzaki Nyogen Sensei used to begin his talks by saying, "Bodhisattvas," as another speaker in his time would have said, "Ladies and Gentlemen."

Learning to accept the role of the Bodhisattva is the nature of Buddhist practice. Avalokiteshvara is not just a figure on the altar. He or she is sitting on your chair as you read this. When you accept your merciful and compassionate tasks in a modest spirit, you walk the path of the Buddha. When the members of the Zen Buddhist center act together as Bodhisattvas, they generate great power for social change —this is the sangha as the Buddha intended it to be.

The *Hua-yen* Sutra refines our understanding of the Bodhisattva role in presenting the doctrine of interpenetration: that I and all beings perfectly reflect and indeed *are* all people, animals, plants, and so on. The metaphor is the "Net of Indra," a model of the universe in which each point of the net is a jewel that perfectly reflects all other jewels. This model is made intimate in Zen study, beginning with our examination of the Buddha's own experience on seeing the Morning Star, when he exclaimed, "I and all beings have at this moment attained the way."[7]

You are at ease with yourself when Kanjizai sits on your cushions—at ease with the world when Kanzeon listens through the hairs of your ears. You are open to the song of the thrush and to the curse of the harlot—like Blake, who knew intimately the interpenetration of things:

> I wander thro' each charter'd street
> Near where the charter'd Thames does flow,
> And mark in every face I meet
> Marks of weakness, marks of woe.
>
> In every cry of every Man,
> In every Infant's cry of fear,
> In every voice, in every ban,
> The mind-forg'd manacles I hear.
>
> How the Chimney-sweeper's cry
> Every black'ning Church appals;
> And the hapless Soldier's sigh
> Runs in blood down Palace walls.
>
> But most thro' midnight streets I hear
> How the youthful Harlot's curse
> Blasts the new born Infant's tear,
> And blights with plagues the Marriage hearse.[8]

We are all of us interrelated—not just people, but animals too, and stones, clouds, trees. And, as Blake wrote so passionately, what a mess we have made of the precious net of relationships. We rationalize ourselves into insensitivity about people, animals, and plants, forging manacles of the mind, confining ourselves to fixed concepts of *I* and *you*, *we* and *it*, birth and death, being and time. This is suffering and distress. But if you can see that all phenomena are transparent, ephemeral, and indeed altogether void, then

the thrush will sing in your heart, and you can suffer with
the prostitute.

Experiencing emptiness is also experiencing peace, and
the potential of peace is its unfolding as harmony among all
people, animals, plants, and things. The precepts formulate this harmony, showing how the absence of killing and
stealing is the very condition of mercy and charity.

This is the Middle Way of Mahayana Buddhism. It is
unself-conscious, and so avoids perfectionism. It is unselfish, and so avoids hedonism. Perfection is the trap of literal
attachment to concepts. A priest from Southeast Asia ex-
plained to us at Koko An, many years ago, that his practice
consisted solely of reciting his precepts, hundreds and hundreds of them. To make his trip to the United States, he had
to receive special dispensation in order to handle money and
talk to women. Surely this was a case of perfectionism.

Hedonism, on the other hand, is the trap of ego-indul-
gence that will not permit any kind of censor, overt or internal, to interfere with self-gratification. The sociopath,
guided only by strategy to get his or her own way, is the
extreme model of such a person. Certain walks of life are full
of sociopaths, but all of us can relate to that condition. Notice how often you manipulate other people. Where is your
compassion?

In the study of the precepts, compassion is seen to have
two aspects, benevolence and reverence. Benevolence, when
stripped of its patronizing connotations, is simply our love
for those who need our love. Reverence, when stripped of
its passive connotations, is simply our love for those who
express their love to us.

The model of benevolence would be the love of parent
toward child, and the model of reverence would be the love
of child toward parent. However, a child may feel benevolence toward parents, and parents reverence toward chil-

dren. Between husband and wife, or friend and friend, these models of compassion are always in flux, sometimes mixed, sometimes exchanged.

Seeing compassion in this detail enables us to understand love as it is, the expression of deepest consciousness directed in an appropriate manner. Wu-men uses the expression, "The sword that kills; the sword that gives life," [9] in describing the compassionate action of a great teacher. On the one hand there is love that says, "Don't do that!" And on the other hand, there is the love that says, "Do as you think best." It is the same love, now "killing" and now "giving life." To one friend we may say, "That's fine." To another we may say, "That won't do." The two actions involved might be quite similar, but in our wisdom perhaps we can discern when to wield the negative, and when the positive.

Without this single, realized mind, corruption can appear. I am thinking of a teacher from India who is currently very popular. I know nothing about him except his many books. His writings sparkle with genuine insight. Yet something is awry. There are sordid patches of anti-Semitism and sexism. Moreover, he does not seem to caution his students about cause and effect in daily life. What went wrong here? I think he chose a short cut to teaching. My impression is that he underwent a genuine religious experience, but missed taking the vital, step-by-step training which in Zen Buddhist tradition comes after realization. Chao-chou trained for over sixty years before he began to teach—a sobering example for us all. The religious path begins again with an experience of insight, and we must train diligently thereafter to become mature.

One of my students taught me the Latin maxim, *In corruptio optima pessima*, "In corruption, the best becomes the worst." For the teacher of religious practice, the opportunity to exploit students increases with his or her charisma and power of expression. Students become more and more open and trusting. The fall of such a teacher is thus a catastrophe that can bring social and psychological breakdown in the sangha.

This is not only a violation of common decency but also of the world view that emerges from deepest experience. You and I come forth as possibilities of essential nature, alone and independent as stars, yet reflecting and being reflected by all things. My life and yours are the unfolding realization of total aloneness and total intimacy. The self is completely autonomous, yet exists only in resonance with all other selves.

Yün-men said, "Medicine and sickness mutually correspond. The whole universe is medicine. What is the self?"[10] I know of no koan that points more directly to the Net of Indra. Yun-men is engaged in the unfolding of universal realization, showing the interchange of self and other as a process of universal health. To see this clearly, you must come to answer Yun-men's question, "What is the self?"

Do you say there is no such thing? Who is saying that, after all! How do you account for the individuality of your manner, the uniqueness of your face? The sixteen Bodhisattva precepts bring Yun-men's question into focus and give it context, the universe and its phenomenon. But while the crackerbarrel philosopher keeps context outside, Yun-men is not such a fellow.

Still, cultural attitudes must be given their due. As Western Buddhists, we are also Judeo-Christian in outlook, perhaps without knowing it. Inevitably we take the precepts differently, just as the Japanese took them differently when they received them from China, and the Chinese differently when Bodhidharma appeared. Where we would say a person is alcoholic, the Japanese will say, "He likes saké very much." The addiction is the same, the suffering is the same, and life is cut short in the same way. But the precept about substance-abuse will naturally be applied one way by Japanese, and another by Americans.

It is also important to trace changes in Western society toward traditional matters over the past twenty years. The Western Zen student is usually particularly sensitive to these changes. Christian and Judaic teachings may seem thin, and nineteenth-century ideals that led people so proudly to celebrate Independence Day and to cheer the Stars and Stripes have all but died out.

I don't dream about the President any more, and when I talk to my friends, I find they don't either. The Great Leader is a hollow man, the Law of the Market cannot prove itself, and the Nation State mocks its own values.

This loss of old concepts and images gives us unprecedented freedom to make use of fundamental virtues, "grandmother wisdom" of conservation, proportion, and decency, to seek the source of rest and peace that has no East or West. It is not possible to identify this source specifically in words —the Zen teacher Seung Sahn calls it the "Don't-Know Mind." He and I and all people who write and speak about Buddhism use Buddhist words and personages to identify that place, yet such presentations continually fall in upon themselves and disappear. We take our inspiration from the *Diamond Sutra* and other sutras of the Prajnaparamita tradition, which stress the importance of not clinging to concepts, even of Buddhahood. [11]

Wu-tsu said, "Shakyamuni and Maitreya are servants of another. I want to ask you, 'Who is that other?'" [12] After you examine yourself for a response to this question, you might want the Buddha and his colleagues to stay around and lend a hand. Perhaps they can inspire your dreams, and

their words express your deepest aspirations; but if they are true servants, they will vanish any time they get in the way.

We need archetypes, as our dreams tell us, to inspire our lives. As lay people together, we do not have the model of a priest as a leader, but we follow in the footsteps of a few great lay personages from Vimalakirti to our own Yamada Roshi, who manifest and maintain the Dharma while nurturing a family.

The sixteen Bodhisattva precepts, too, are archetypes, "skillful means" for us to use in guiding our engagement with the world. They are not commandments engraved in stone, but expressions of inspiration written in something more fluid than water. Relative and absolute are altogether blended. Comments on the precepts by Bodhidharma and Dogen Zenji are studied as koans, but our everyday life is a great, multifaceted koan that we resolve at every moment, and yet never completely resolve.[13]

CHAPTER TWO

The First
Grave Precept
Not Killing

The Ten Grave Precepts are negatively framed, but actually, like the Ten Commandments of Judeo-Christian tradition, they are not interpreted negatively or positively, but
as presentations of compassionate wisdom that uses "negative and positive," "right and wrong" sensibly and de-
cently. The First Precept plainly means "Don't kill," but it
also expresses social concern: "Let us encourage life," and it
relates to the mind: "There is no thought of killing."

There are the three elements that the Zen teacher uses in
conveying the precepts: the literal, the compassionate, and
the essential, or, as they are more technically termed: the
Hinayana, the Mahayana, and the Buddha-nature views.
Hinayana and Mahayana should not be confused in this
usage with sectarian or geographical classifications. They
refer to attitudes, not necessarily to beliefs of people living
in Sri Lanka or Japan.

The Hinayana view of "Not Killing" is just that. The
extreme limit of such literal interpretation is not Buddhist
at all, but the Jain faith, whose monks filter all water before drinking it, in order to protect the microscopic animals that might otherwise be swallowed. I am not familiar

enough with Jain theology to know just how ahimsa (not harming) really works for its followers. They must assume that a sharp distinction exists between the animal and vegetable worlds; otherwise they could not feed themselves. Strict vegetarians, too, tend to fall into this trap, it seems to me. It is not possible to evade the natural order of things: everything in the universe is in symbiosis with every other thing.

> Great fleas have lesser fleas, upon their backs to bite 'em,
> And little fleas have lesser fleas, and so *ad infinitum*.[1]

The industrialist says, "It's a dog-eat-dog world." The Bodhisattva, taking the Mahayana view, does not deny the fact, only the spirit of such an aphorism. He or she follows the way of compassion, nurturing all beings and being nurtured by them.

The Buddha-nature view is summed up in the *Heart Sutra* "There is no old age and death, and also no ending of old age and death."[2] It is important to see into this passage clearly. The first point is that in the world of nirvana, the real world of empty infinity, there is nothing to be called death. From this point of view, Takuan Zenji is right: there is no one killing, no killing, and no one to be killed. The peace of infinite emptiness pervades the universe.

I discussed the risks of this absolute position, when taken exclusively, in "The Nature of the Precepts." If there is no sword, no swing of the sword, no decapitation, then what about all the blood? What about the wails of the widow and children? The absolute position, when isolated, omits human details completely. Doctrines, including Buddhism, are meant to be used. Beware of them taking life of their own, for then they use us. Nirvana, the purity and clarity of the void, is the name we give to the total peace one experiences in deepest realization. But that is the same sea that we experience rising and falling in samsara, the relative world of coming and going. We cannot abstract depth from surface, nor surface from depth. Killing, even in an exalted state of mind, cannot be separated from suffering. The nirvana realized in Zen practice is "right here before our eyes," as Hakuin Zenji says in his "Song of Zazen." [3] It is not something abstract. Leaves are green—flowers are red; we stand up and sit down, die and are born, and though this very place is the Lotus Land, the Lotus Land is also this very place.

Practicing compassion goes hand in hand with practicing realization. On your cushions in the dojo (the training center) you learn first of all to be compassionate toward yourself. I can recall occasions when I sat in zazen with my mind a turmoil of murderous thoughts and feelings. Perhaps you have had such experiences also. We vow to save all beings, but how do you save the roughnecks in your own mind? Treat them as neighbors who come to the door when you are meditating. Take a moment to acknowledge them. They are closer than neighbors, after all.

"Oh, there you are, you violent thought." With this recognition, you are Kanjizai, at ease with yourself because you are no longer blindly responsive to your thinking and feeling—and thus no longer at the mercy of your karma. Then when your boss or somebody else takes up a role in the old family play that formed your life, you can exclaim, "Oh, I remember you!" and the pain will be reduced. You will be left to deal with circumstances, which might be difficult enough without clouds of childish emotions to confuse them. This Bodhisattva practice has its source in zazen where you discern the power of a single unacknowledged thought (it carries you away), and the importance of seeing through it.

Thoughts and feelings conveyed from our grandparents and beyond disrupt our families and set the stage for the continuation of subtle and even overt violence in the future. With awareness, all this can change.

"I should not have said [or done] that," you can say to your spouse or child, and the damage is repaired to some degree, perhaps without a seam if it is caught soon enough. Compulsion is weakened by such correction, and next time perhaps the error will be milder. This too is Bodhisattva practice. Complete freedom and devoted compassion are the same in the Buddha-mind, but even Shakyamuni had to work at it. He did not experience true nature as soon as he sat down, after all.

There are collective thoughts and feelings too—national compulsions. These days we are pressed to come up with rationalizations that do violence to all three views of "Not Killing." Distinguished social philosophers labor to define the "just war." Entire countries, entire cultures are killed for so-called pragmatic reasons, which we cannot deny without destroying basic assumptions, such as the virtue of the nation-state. We are shown statistics of war and peace down through the ages, and with a sigh we are obliged to agree that the world has made far more war than peace. For the Buddhist, however, it is not possible to move from the integrated position set forth in the First Precept. Just because historical statistics show lots of war, it does not follow that behind history there is an imperative to wage war. Indeed, the imperative is self-realization. It is the perversion of self-realization into self-aggrandizement that directs the course of our lives to violence. The fundamental fact is that I cannot survive unless you do. My self-realization is your self-realization.

The collective ego of the nation-state is subject to the same poisons of greed, hatred, and ignorance as the individual. We have reached the place in international affairs, and in local affairs too, where it is altogether absurd to insist, as some of my Buddhist friends still do, that the religious person does not get involved in politics. What is political? Is torture political? As a matter of fact, the denial of politics in religious life is itself a political statement. The time when politics meant taking a position of allegiance to one government faction or another has long passed. Politics in our day of nuclear overkill is a matter of ignoring the First Precept or acting upon it.

Acting upon the First Precept is also the spirit of not harming applied in the natural world. The same poisons that set us apart in families, communities, and across national boundaries—greed, hatred, and ignorance—blight the grasslands, deplete the soil, clearcut the forests, and add lethal chemicals to water and air. In the name of progress, some say. In the name of greed, it might more accurately be said. We are killing our world, the web of life and death that realizes Buddha-nature in many forms, evolving to what Mahayana Buddhists call the enlightenment of plants and trees.[4] Animals and plants are mortal beings of the ordinary world, but they are also archetypes that enrich our process of maturing when we are children, and populate our dreams when we are adults. This dreamtime is the true world, traditional people tell us. As human animals we are nightmare figures in that dreamtime for wolves and most other wild creatures. We torture animals in our laboratories under an arrogant set of anthropocentric assumptions, and we divert the grand possibilities of nature into sordid feedlots, reducing animals to machines and degrading their human keepers. The dreamtime is impoverished and miserable.

I do not hold to the perfectionistic position that before one can work for the protection of animals, forests, and small family farms—or for world peace—one must be completely realized, compassionate, and peaceful. There is no end to the process of perfection, and so the perfectionist cannot even begin Bodhisattva work. Compassion and peace are a practice, on cushions in the dojo, within the family, on the job, and at political forums. Do your best with what you have, and you will mature in the process.

There are many personal tests of this practice, from dealing with insects and mice to questions about capital punishment. Perhaps the most intimate and agonizing test is faced by the woman considering abortion. Over-simplified positions of pro-life and pro-choice do not touch the depths of her dilemma. Usually she experiences distressing conflict between her sexual/reproductive drive and the realities of her life: social, economic, and personal—and indeed, she faces such realities for any child she may bring to term.

I have known women who said they were not upset at having an abortion, but I would guess that they were not sensitive to their own feelings at that particular time. Perhaps distress shows up in their dreams. Surely self-awareness is never more important.

Sitting in on sharing meetings in the Diamond Sangha, our Zen Buddhist society in Hawaii, I get the impression that when a woman is sensitive to her feelings, she is conscious that abortion is killing a part of herself and terminating the ancient process, begun anew within herself, of bringing life into being. Thus she is likely to feel acutely miserable after making a decision to have an abortion. This is a time for compassion for the woman, and for her to be compassionate with herself and for her unborn child. If I am consulted, and we explore the options carefully and I learn that the decision is definite, I encourage her to go through the act with the consciousness of a mother who holds her dying child in her arms, lovingly nurturing it as it passes from life. Sorrow and suffering form the nature of samsara, the flow of life and death, and the decision to prevent birth is made on balance with other elements of suffering. Once the decision is made, there is no blame, but rather acknowledgment that sadness pervades the whole universe, and this bit of life goes with our deepest love.

In Japanese Buddhism, there is a funeral service for the *mizuko* ("water baby," the poetical term for fetus). Like any other human being that passes into the One, it is given a posthumous Buddhist name, and is thus identified as an individual, however incomplete, to whom we can say farewell. With this ceremony, the woman is in touch with life and death as they pass through her existence, and she finds that such basic changes are relative waves on the great ocean of true nature, which is not born and does not pass away. (See the Appendix, p. 175.)

> Bodhidharma said, "Self-nature is subtle and mysterious. In the realm of the everlasting Dharma, not giving rise to concepts of killing is called the Precept of Not Killing."

"Self-nature" can be understood to be a synonym for "essential nature" and there is a reason for having the two terms. The "self" portion, pronounced *ji* in Sino-Japanese, is the *ji* of Kanjizai, the one who perceives the self at rest. Kanjizai as you or me has no thought of killing. The self at rest is essential nature as we experience it, and so we call it self-nature. It is subtle and mysterious, the Buddha-mind that pervades the whole universe, realized as the potent self of no-substance.

"Concepts" is literally "views" in the original. "Opinions" might be another translation. "Not giving rise to" is literally "not giving birth to." No concept of killing is born, in other words.

Bodhidharma takes the essential position and is not referring to means. The practice of peace and harmony *is*
peace and harmony, not some technique designed to induce
them. In the family, "Not Killing" means giving total attention to spouse and children, and gaining a deep sense of
how they feel. Male and female have different perspectives;
children and adults live in different worlds. Without falling into a kind of pernicious equality in which all views are
equally valid, you can play with views and see what happens. If I am anxious to protect myself, then I will kill your
views. If I practice giving life, then I will offer you the scope
you need.

Even deeply held convictions can melt in the dynamics of
give and take where male and female, adult and child,
friend and friend hold dialogue in a spirit of trust. Easier
said than done, to be sure, but the path of lazy retreat leads
inevitably to suffering.

Even dangerous views can be entertained in dialogue,
with trust that their full exploration will reveal their danger. This is the virtue of street theater in peace demonstra-
tions. The views of the other are taken to their extremity,
and when creatively presented the effect is a mirror to reality. In effect, this is "killing the views" of the other, but the
motive is ahimsa, not harming, and there is no thought of
taking life.

Dialogue is the Tao. In Zen Buddhism this is the *mondō*,
questions and answers between teacher and student or
student and student, striking sparks that neither creates
alone. With no thought of killing, our cause is peaceful and
harmonious. Down through the decades of peace and environmental work in this century, from Satyagraha to the
Movement for a New Society, we find leaders holding fast to
peace itself. They turn the wheel of the Dharma of peace,

using means that are themselves expressive and instructive. When we convey the truth in this way to people who hold concepts of violence, then compassion is not compromised.

"Speaking truth to power," the ideal of the Society of Friends, is nonviolent and inclusive. Recently, leaders of a peace organization arranged to meet with a senior military officer who had broad authority. I don't know why he agreed to meet with them, and I did not hear the outcome of the meeting. I was just told about discussions in the organization before the meeting took place. The delegation had to decide what to say. After role-playing several scenarios, the members gave up and decided just to open the conversation with the question, "How is it going?" In other words, with your truly awesome power, with nuclear war a possible outcome of something you might decide to do in an emergency, how are you bearing up? When we speak from the same side of the counter in this way, then we are human beings together; the we-they dichotomy falls away, and peace has a chance.

This peace is not the vacuum of a sensory-deprivation chamber, or the harmony created by authority. It is the peace of the self forgotten, doing the work of the world.

Dogen Zenji said, "The Buddha-seed grows in accordance with not taking life. Transmit the life of Buddha's wisdom and do not kill."

Dogen Zenji is a kindly grandmother, petting us and giving us encouragement. With the practice of not killing, he is saying, you will become the Buddha and transmit his wisdom. We can only be grateful for his guidance on the true path.

Bodhidharma takes an absolute position of unrelenting purity and Dogen Zenji offers a step-by-step way of practice. The practical way to practice not-harming begins with a lifestyle that acknowledges all the implications of popular Western culture, and popular Eastern culture too, these days. When I look at my camera, and in tiny print I read, "Made in Singapore," I reflect upon the women who are employed at the factory there for low wages, who have no room in their lives for anything creative. I reflect upon the American workers who have no jobs because the factory has moved to Asia. There is no quick remedy for this injustice, but awareness is the beginning of Right Action. Gathering information and publishing it spreads awareness. Then when the facts are in, the options for action become clear. And the action is effective because the synergy of group effort spreads awareness even further.

When I listen to children, I realize how intimately they are caught up in popular (violent) culture. Here too, there is no quick remedy. Parents are caught in a painful dilemma, for they know the power of TV and schoolyard influences, and the risk of isolating themselves with well-meant cautions. Again, the sangha is our treasure, for it can provide a setting that will nurture Right Views. It is important to join together to work out specific means for this cultivation.

For me, all this begins with zazen. Translate "zazen" as "meditation" in Christian or other religious practice, if you like. I am not seeking to convince anybody that Zen Buddhism is the only possible path. However, true meditation, whatever the lineage, is not just a matter of sitting quietly. During that time on one's cushions, everything in the universe disappears, and the peace one experiences is eternal peace.

Each of us finds inspiration with particular symbols and archetypes. When I bought the Bodhidharma figure that presides at the Koko An Zendo (our Zen hall in Honolulu), his brother Dogen was for sale in the same bookstore window in Tokyo. I bought only one half of the pair. Somewhere the teacher of the path is leading another group of friends, perhaps. I take it as my responsibility as a Zen teacher to evoke Dogen Zenji in my heart, and to encourage you to evoke him in yours, to practice giving life, inspired by Bodhidharma's great example and succinct expression of truth. But whatever one's way of life—peace in manner, peace in words, peace in speaking truth to the power of greed and cruelty in the world, all have their source in rigorous religious practice.

CHAPTER THREE

The Second
Grave Precept

Not Stealing

Many years ago I was down and out in Los Angeles, working in Everybody's Bookshop at the corner of 8th and Hope for $1.15 per hour, and living in the nearby YMCA. Sometimes I would drop into a bar for a couple of beers after supper, and on one of those occasions, a well-dressed middle-aged man sat down beside me, very drunk, flashing a wallet that was stuffed with bills. The bartender served him a drink, and then told him to go home and take care of his money. The man told me that he was from Sacramento, and asked me to help him find his way back to his hotel.

I escorted him to the hotel, which was just down the block, and then, because he had difficulty walking, I saw him up to his room, and even walked in with him, as he seemed to be getting sick. He used the bathroom, came out, and without a word, removed his gold cufflinks, took out his gold watch and his wallet, put them all on the dresser, changed to his pajamas, crawled into bed, and fell sound asleep, leaving me to make my way out of the hotel alone.

I was not tempted to steal his valuables. But I wonder now whether that was because I was morally strong or sim-

27

ply afraid to commit a robbery. Certainly, I fantasized for months afterwards about that wallet on the dresser, bulging with one-hundred-dollar bills. It would have been so easy to help myself to a year's wages. It can be said that in my mind I violated the Second Precept many times during the months that followed.

Looking back now, I realize that I also stole from myself in the course of the incident. It was generous of me to guide the drunken man back to his hotel, but it was reckless to accompany him any further than the lobby. I might better have raised a finger to the night man as I passed the desk, and the hotel people would have seen my companion to bed. Quite unnecessarily, I was putting myself, the agent of compassion, in jeopardy. I was endangering my capacity to help others at a later time, for suppose the drunken man had made some sort of fuss while we were alone in his room, and perhaps falsely accused me of something. If I am to have a police record, let it be for something I can confidently justify from the ground of my dojo.

There are many ways of stealing from oneself, some of them in the dojo itself. The theft of time is one. Yamamoto Gempō Roshi used to call this kind of stealing the greatest felony of all. We take time on our cushions to indulge in all kinds of silly business, and the biological clock ticks away relentlessly. We also take time from our lives as Bodhisattvas for all kinds of foolishness, altogether out of proportion to our natural needs for leisure. These are habits, beings with their own life force that we must acknowledge and engage in dialogue.

"Time to sit!" you can announce, "I'll check you later." Fun time with family and friends has its place. Be firm, but be patient, and your time-wasting habits will find their outlet in re-creational activities.

"Back to Mu!"[1] you can announce there on your cushions, and the Old Nick that wants you to steal time for re-arranging the furniture in your apartment will be put on hold. There is an appropriate time for that kind of visualization also.

Still another kind of stealing on your cushions lies in the attitude of expectation. Practice is a step-by-step process, the perfection of character, as Yamada Roshi has said, but each step is full and complete. When your attention is on your series of steps and their goal, then the goal is never reached, and your life is wasted. Each breath, each Mu—that is the Dharma body itself. Don't deprive yourself.

"Not stealing," like other precepts, describes the mind, which comes forth from a position of rest:

> Bodhidharma said, "Self-nature is subtle and mysterious. In the realm of the unattainable Dharma, not having thoughts of gaining is called the Precept of Not Stealing."

Mind is peace, and because it is peace, it is also broad and generous. There is no thought of obtaining, so there is full appreciation for the thing as it is.

> Dogen Zenji said, "The self and the things of the world are just as they are. The gate of emancipation is open."

"Just as they are" is the realization, "Wow! That wallet is stuffed with one-hundred-dollar bills!" There is no thought in that moment or later of putting them into my pocket. This is the broad and generous spirit of letting be, the perfection of charity or giving over, the *Dānapāramitā*. It is also the revolution that overturns conventional behavior.

Stealing is a pervasive element of our lives, and is the nature of our economic system. "The rich get rich and the poor get poorer." To take an extreme example, a large American corporation raises vegetables in the Sahel, near the Sahara Desert. These vegetables are flown to Europe, where they fill the salad bowls of the affluent. The African workers on this giant farm, whose families and friends live at the edge of starvation, are searched at the end of each day to be sure they are not smuggling vegetables home. Yet the corporation land they cultivate was once their own for gleaning and grazing.

We don't notice similar examples nearer home because we are used to them, but our slums and skid rows are clear symptoms of an economy that is manipulated here and abroad to provide a base of unemployment so that competition for jobs will keep wages at a minimum, and stockholders will realize maximum profits. The natural world is exploited for short-term benefit to a "fortunate" minority, while other people, animals, plants, and the earth organism itself suffer.

At the same time, exploitation is not something outside my mind or yours. Just a few minutes of television is enough to show each of us how easily we are seduced by appeals for consumption. Mahatma Gandhi says,

> We are not always aware of our real needs, and most of us improperly multiply our wants, and thus unconsciously make thieves of ourselves. If we devote some thought to the subject, we shall find that we can get rid of quite a number of our wants. One who follows the observance of Non-stealing will bring about a progressive reduction of his own wants. Much of the distressing poverty in this world has arisen out of the breaches of the principle of Non-stealing.[2]

Notice that Gandhi does not speak of reducing possessions, though that would naturally follow, and certainly did in his own case. He speaks of reducing needs, and needs arise in the mind. Our world faces the gravest of crises because we have all of us become involved in a conspiracy to

deplete irreplaceable resources in order to satisfy needs established in that very depletion process. As time goes on, oil and minerals will become scarcer, and the kind of brutality evident in my example from the Sahel may become more commonplace, at home as well as abroad. Unto Tähtinen says,

> There are two ways of avoiding war: one is to satisfy everyone's desire, the other, to content oneself with the good. The former is not possible due to the limitations of the world and therefore there remains this second alternative of contentment.[3]

"Not Stealing" is contentment, no thought of obtaining. This starts much deeper in the mind than deciding to do without luxuries. It is none other than the open gate of emancipation, *anuttara-samyak-sambodhi*, the mind that experiences the transparency of all things and their intimate interrelationships. The application of this experience is more than the sending of an occasional check to charity. Here again Gandhi is instructive:

> In India we have got three million people who have to be satisfied with one meal a day, and that meal consisting of a chapati containing no fat in it, and a pinch of salt. You and I have no right to anything that we . . . have until these three millions are clothed and fed better. You and I, who ought to know better, must adjust our wants, and even undergo voluntary starvation in order that they may be nursed, fed and clothed.[4]

And, as Gandhi made clear in his own life, it is in the social movement to reduce needs that there is hope for political change. Our Zen groups can become danaparamita sanghas.

Some people suppose that because competition and acquisition are used in the exploitation of others, enlightened people should seek the ideal of noncompetition and nonacquisition. Many years ago, Anne Aitken and I taught in a private boarding school that was established upon the principle of noncompetition. It didn't work. The young people were not stretched; many became lazy; others found destructive, underground ways of competing. Competition *can* be healthy. After all, conversation itself is a kind of competition, and at its best in Zen dialogues it saves all beings. When the self is forgotten, the play becomes the thing, and everybody benefits. And as to acquisition, Gandhi and the Buddha himself had a few possessions. Competition sharpens our realization, and certain possessions are adjuncts of life. At what point do they go wrong?

In Japan, monks are known as *unsui*, "cloud and water," and the implication is that they have no home, no ego needs, and no attachments. In fact, however, they have a few possessions: a couple of anthologies of classic Zen cases, a set of bowls, toilet articles, and robes, much as the Buddha did. When I visited Ryūtaku Monastery in 1964, I found that the sangha was upset by the presence of a new monk who was stealing the few possessions of the other monks. Each day, the senior monks held long meetings with the Roshi to discuss the problem. I imagine the literal position, "He violated the Second Precept," and the absolute position, "There is no stealing and nothing to be stolen" were argued in these meetings, but the outcome was the Middle Way of compassion. A year later, I visited the monastery again, and found the monk still there, now free of his problems, and the community at peace.

I suggest that such a difficult problem could not have been worked out if the monks had not realized that the thief was someone deprived of love, and that he stole to share what belonged to others in a kind of perverse loyalty. *Dāna* ("charity") in this case was the acknowledgment of responsibility to a confused fellow-monk, as well as to personal things. "You are my brother, and I love you," each monk was somehow able to say, in effect at least. Thus a pathological, destructive drive for love was corrected, with no thought of stealing or protecting, and the Tao was made real.

Competition, acquisition, and possession go wrong when compassion is missing, when dana is disregarded. Chaochou polished his realization in Dharma-combat for twenty years in order to prepare himself as an instrument of compassion, declaring generously at the outset that he was open to the teaching of even a seven-year-old child. Thus he became one of the greatest Zen teachers.

Acquisition and possession are generous when the state of mind is "Just as it is." The teacher of tea experiences the tea bowl and bows to the venerable kettle, but these days there are few such teachers, and the tea ceremony is often just a kind of show, with its religious function forgotten. Rainer Maria Rilke deplores this same loss in European culture:

> Even for our grandparents, a "house," a "well," a familiar tower, their very clothes, their coat: were infinitely more, infinitely more intimate; almost everything a vessel in which they found the human and added to the store of the human. Now, from America, empty indifferent things are pouring across, sham things, *dummy life*. . . . A house, in the American sense, an American apple or grapevine over there, has *nothing* in common with the house, the fruit, the grape into which went the hopes and reflections of our forefathers. . . . Live things, things lived and conscient of us, are running out, and can no longer be replaced. *We are perhaps the last still to have known such things*. On us rests the responsibility not alone of preserving *their* memory (that

would be too little and unreliable), but their human and laral value. ("Laral" in the sense of household gods.)⁵

"Pots and pans are Buddha's body," announces a sign in some Zen Buddhist monasteries, reminding the cooks of "Just as they are." *Zafus* ("cushions") and blankets, hammers and shovels, all are Buddha's body. I confess I am offended when I see zoris left every which way at the temple door, when I see someone straighten his cushion with his foot, when I see tools left in the rain. Things are altogether faithful. They follow the rules with precision. We owe them benevolence in return.

Carelessness with precious things is a kind of stealing, but so is the greed of the collector. Once, Nakagawa Sōen Roshi, Anne Aitken, and I visited a Buddhist teacher and healer in Honolulu. She was a remarkable personage, very charismatic, with a large, devoted following, and a magnificent temple. But her preoccupation with money flawed her character, and every day she violated the Second Precept. Knowing that we enjoyed tea ceremony, this teacher led us to her treasury, where there were a hundred tea bowls in boxes on shelves along one wall. She took down several, removed them from their boxes, unwrapped them one by one for our admiration, and each time she asked, "How much do you suppose that one cost?" And then, breaking the silence, she would tell us: so many tens of thousands of yen. With such static in our ears, it was difficult to come forth and say, each time, "What a beautiful bowl!"

Tea ceremony carried within itself the seeds of its own ruin from the very beginning, for it was a way of poverty for the rich. On the other hand, Zen Buddhism in Asia is dying because its particular way of purity no longer affects the larger community. In the Buddha's time, and down through the ages until a century and a half ago, the world outside the monastery walls just *was*—despots and benevolent rulers rose and fell, and the individual dealing with personal difficulties could come to the monastery for a retreat, or to become a monk or nun.

Today the delusions of greed, hatred, and ignorance fuel industrial and political systems that threaten the very structure of life. Air, water, and food are depleted and poisoned, and the machine of death and destruction accelerates. The dojo has always been a retreat and a training center, but now the emphasis must be upon training ourselves as a danaparamita community to become a new growth within the shell of the old society. To begin with, this is the perfection of charity within our own sangha as we take care of each other and encourage each other. Unresolved conflicts within the sangha interrupt the flow of love at its source, and mock our volunteer programs in the community. With harmony among ourselves, however, we can find inspiration in the broad sky of *samādhi* and in the way the Buddha showed his bowl in the world.

The Buddha was a wandering saint, and his very presence brought peace to those who met him. Ahimsa was a personal way of life for his sangha, but the Buddha's day is not ours, and we can learn from Gandhi how ancient teachings of nonviolence can be applied in our world of imperialism.

We can also learn from and join with other communities of compassion in our own time, groups with concerns that range from civil liberties to peace to ecology, groups that are, in effect, already teaching danaparamita. Buddhist danaparamita communities are in the vanguard of a nonviolent movement for social change along with Christians, Jews, and humanists.

But Bodhidharma and Dogen Zenji delineate the special contribution that Buddhist communities may offer. The broad and generous state of mind that gives rise to dana-paramita is the realm of "vast emptiness; nothing holy" and the human condition of the "fallen-away body and mind." It is the dojo of emptiness, the formless ground where the tea bowl is realized as just that tea bowl, in itself and in symbiosis with every element of the universe, including oneself. In practical, everyday terms, it is where we take care of our friends.

This is the miracle of ordinary life for everybody now, for the dojo is at last my home, your home, and the sangha is our community that flows outward in limitless circles from our center of peace. This very place is the Lotus Land, right now, and not yet—and the "not yet" is our action of bowing to each other and seating ourselves on our zafus, and our work of showing the Dharma in a world of crisis.

CHAPTER FOUR

The Third
Grave Precept

Not Misusing Sex

The original title of this precept is "No Unrighteous Lewdness" (a kind of tautology, which in Chinese—and in older English—can be a strong expression). "Lewdness" has a rather quaint ring in modern English, but its derivation is instructive. It comes from an Old English word meaning "unlearned," implying boorish. No boorish sex. That's a good precept for us all.

What did our Zen Buddhist ancestors say about sex? In my directory of some 5,500 koans, I find no entry for this subject in the elaborate index.[1] I do know of one pertinent koan, however, and although it is tainted by stereotyped views toward women, it also rebukes the puritanical attitudes commonly associated with religion, East and West:

In ancient days, an old woman gave housing and food to a hermit over a period of twenty years. One day she sent her sixteen-year-old niece to take food to the hermit, telling her to make advances to him to see what he would do. The girl laid her head on the hermit's lap, and said, "How is this?"

The hermit said, "The withered tree is rooted in an ancient rock in bitter cold. During the winter months, there is no warmth, no life."

The girl reported this to her aunt. The old woman said,
"That vulgarian! To think that I have made offerings to him
for twenty years!" She drove away the hermit and burned
down his cottage.[2]

While we may question the use of the niece as bait to test
the monk's realization, it is clear by the final response of the
aunt that fundamentally she too disapproves of the misuse
of sex. The hermit was not responding to the human being
who laid her head in his lap. He was using her to express his
own ascetic position.

So the aunt calls him a vulgarian, a boor. Lewdness is
boorish; asceticism can be, and often is, boorish. Boorish-
ness is thinking just of one's self. She drives him off and
burns down his cottage. Fire is a dream symbol for sex.
"You don't belong here! Sex belongs here!" Or at least acknowledgment of it.

This case is listed under "Offerings to Monks" in my directory of koans, and the lack of any classification for sex is
in keeping with the curtain that is drawn over the subject in
Zen.[3] After a careful search of the literature, you can find
cautions by Dogen Zenji to avoid sexual gossip, but that is
about all, except, of course, this precept and its brief commentaries. In the Zen monastery food, sleep, zazen, work,
and even going to the toilet are organized and scheduled,
but it is as though sex does not exist. I am not so naive as to
suppose that this could be possible, but I must say that the
mildest kind of homosexual fooling around among young
monks was all the sex I ever observed in several months of
residence in a Japanese Zen monastery.

The case of the aunt and the hermit is not included in the
anthologies of koans chosen for Zen study by Harada Dai'un
Roshi, but it is generally part of the Rinzai curriculum.
Even so, one wonders how students can apply its teaching.

In Japanese Zen monasteries today, women are admitted for
sesshin (retreats) only, as a general rule. They sit in a separate
room, and only join the men for meals, sutras, and teishos,
and even then they are grouped together. At teisho time,
the laymen sit with the monks, and the women sit on the
other side of the room with guests who come in from outside especially to hear the talk. The message is clearly,
"Zazen is for men."

Japanese generally place the onus of sexual distraction
upon women. At least until very recently, Japanese boys
and girls mingled very little in their teenage years, and the
monk who went off at eighteen to train in a monastery
would simply not be able to handle the presence of a woman
in the dojo. Her appearance would prompt long-repressed
sexual urges to take over his zazen—Mu would disappear,
and the result would be failure in the *dokusan* ("interview")
room and disruption of the monastic routine.

The roshi, sitting at the heart of the Zen training program, is not likely to be interested in trying to make over
the society that presents him with this problem. Within his
own milieu, he solves it in the only way that seems to him to
be possible, by excluding and segregating the immediate
"cause." This is a negative model for us in Western Zen, and
as such it can be very instructive.

Senzaki Nyogen Sensei liked the story of the nun Eshun,
who, it seems, did practice with a sangha of monks:

> Twenty monks and one nun, who was named Eshun, were
> practicing meditation under a certain Zen master. Eshun
> was very pretty, even though her head was shaved and her
> dress plain. Several monks secretly fell in love with her, and
> one of them wrote her a love letter, insisting on a private
> meeting.
>
> Eshun did not reply. The following day, the master gave a
> teisho to the group, and when it was over, Eshun stood and

faced the monk who had written her and said, "If you really love me so much, come and embrace me now."[4]

One of my students remarked that Eshun's action was self-righteous. I am not so sure. In her context, perhaps it was quite appropriate. In modern circumstances, we seek to be honest in such matters, and can appreciate her intention. In any case, if you were the monk, how would you reply to her challenge?

In discussing this matter with students, I said that I would go over to her and make a bow, or in our society, offer to shake her hand. One student said, "If I were the monk, I'd go over and embrace her." This is a Zen-like response, but also very modern and Western.

So far as I know, all the Zen centers in the United States today accommodate both men and women. This arrangement, like ordinary life away from the center, brings a stream of crises that hinge on sex. In the dokusan room, you may be asked about the aunt and the hermit. The question is, "In that situation, how would you respond as the hermit to the niece?" Like all good koans, this one is neat and tidy, and only one sort of response is possible. However, the acid test of the mime in the dokusan room is the act itself thereafter. Here you are in your friend's apartment. The circumstances are thus and so. How do you respond in such a time and place, with this person? No dithering allowed!

The acid test is also found in the Western Zen Buddhist training center, where men and women not only sit side by side in the dojo, but also eat together, work together, sometimes bathe together. How do such arrangements affect their Zen training? How is their Zen training applied to these circumstances?

Though there are many problems, I think the overall effect of such proximity is beneficial to the practice. There is an experience of wholeness in having the other sex in close association throughout the day. Fantasies about sex are still present, but surely are less fierce than they might be if there were no chance to experience the humanity of the other in the give and take of cooking, gardening, and reroofing together. In this dimension, one is better able to accept the thoughts as normal and natural, and permit them to pass. There are tensions in a coeducational community, but there are tensions in celibate communities as well. People in combination produce tensions. Tensions can be used creatively, or one can be used by them.

The sexual drive is part of the human path of self-realization. With our modern, relatively permissive sexual mores, we have increased opportunity to explore our human nature through sexual relationships. At the same time, of course, there is more opportunity for self-centered people to use sex as a means for personal power. The path you choose rises from your fundamental purpose. Why are you here?

The roshi in charge of a monastery who avoids difficulties simply by dividing humanity in half had his counterpart in Western Victorian society, where exclusion and segregation were used as a means of control. With the help of our evolving Western cultural attitudes, we in the Zen movement can use sex in our practice, rather than trying to exclude it. I don't mean that we should be experimenting with tantra, but simply that we must acknowledge sexual energy as part of the sangha treasure.

Certainly we cannot justify rejecting sex and accepting the other human drives and emotions, such as anger, fear, hunger, and the need for sleep. All we have learned on our cushions proves that physical and mental conditions, the will, and emotions are human elements to be integrated into our daily-life practice and our zazen practice. For all its ecstatic nature, for all its power, sex is just another human

drive. If we avoid it just because it is more difficult to inte-
grate than anger or fear, then we are simply saying that
when the chips are down we cannot follow our own practice. This is dishonest and unhealthy. According to the
Gnostic Gospel of Thomas, Jesus said,

> If you bring forth what is within you, what you bring forth
> will save you. If you do not bring forth what is within you,
> what you do not bring forth will destroy you.[5]

Be careful. There are many people in prisons and asylums
because they thought God told them to pull the trigger or
wield the axe. The words of world teachers like Jesus and
Buddha are intended to clarify the way of honor.

In the past twenty years in the West, homosexuals have
taken the words of Jesus to heart. On this subject again, we
are on our own. If the old teachers were reticent on the subject of conventional sex, they were altogether silent about
the unconventional. A Japanese Zen monk of my acquaint-
ance became a roshi, and a few months later, looking back
on the counseling sessions he had been holding informally
with his students, both monks and laypeople, he remarked
to me, "I had no idea that homosexuality was so wide-
spread. I thought it was just an occasional problem."

Homosexuality becomes a problem if society and the individuals involved view it as a problem. My feeling is that
with the encouragement of teacher and sangha, the individual member has a chance for personal maturity and realization through Zen practice, whether he or she is hetero-
sexual or homosexual. Buddha nature is not either one and
it is both.

Buddha-nature is, in fact, the essence and quality of energy, including the human energy of sex.

> Bodhidharma said, "Self-nature is subtle and mysterious.
> In the realm of the ungilded Dharma, not creating a veneer
> of attachment is called the Precept of Not Misusing Sex."

Bodhidharma was celibate, of course, and his words were directed to his celibate followers. Celibacy is an appropriate path for some Zen students today, but celibate or not, we can all of us find guidance in Bodhidharma's words. The nonattachment of suchness is the Tao of all the Buddhas. Sasaki Jōshū Roshi has said, "When you are completely one with your lover, you don't know whether you are doing something good or bad." [6] Or attached or nonattached.

> Dogen Zenji said, "The Three Wheels are pure and clear.
> When you have nothing to desire, you follow the way of all
> Buddhas."

The Three Wheels are the actor, the thing acted upon, and the action. Committed lovers and their act of love are intrinsically pure and clear. There is no attainment at all. The celibate too, fully realized, finds that Buddha-nature pervades the whole universe. Bodhidharma and Dogen Zenji shine light on our path, and if little is said about sex specifically in the rest of Zen Buddhist teaching, our way is nonetheless clear. The universe itself guides us with the purity of its vacancy, and with the intimate interreflection of its beings.

Thus when there is an easy drawing together, a new love relationship can be conducive to deeper practice for the sangha. A difficult relationship can also be a field for practice.

However, practice can be disrupted by actions that sangha members perceive as boorish sex. If there is a wolf among the lambs, the practice may be overwhelmed throughout the dojo, as though someone had left the television going during sesshin. And what if the teacher is the wolf? The words of Bodhidharma and Dogen Zenji are simply profound expressions of common morality. It is up to the Zen teacher and his or her senior followers to build a solid road of example and zazen that will link the wisdom of our ancestors to the exigencies of ordinary living.

I am especially concerned about the grave upsets in American Zen Buddhist centers recently that have followed upon affairs of teachers with their students. These cases seem to reflect a misuse, not just of sex, but more generally of the teacher's role in the sangha.

The teacher of religious practice occupies an archetypal place in the psyches of the students. He or she continues to teach in their dreams. This is a factor that must be worked with in teacher-student relations. On the one hand, it is important for the teacher to be responsible for this power, and to encourage the students to use its influence, and to speak out when they think they are being used. On the other hand, it is important for students to avoid blind allegiance. For example, I once challenged a student about sexist and anti-Semitic statements made by his teacher. He replied, "It is true; he is sexist and anti-Semitic. But he is the guru." That won't do, I think.

The function of the teacher is to teach, just as the function of the mother or father is to be a parent, or the function of the psychologist is to counsel. All of these roles set up archetypal responses, and at best such responses are positive and productive. When the teacher, in the role of teacher, confronts a student sexually, the archetype is violated, and the student is deeply confused and disturbed. This is a law, as irrevocable as the Law of Gravity, proved in the suffering of earnest Zen students and their sanghas today.

In this connection, a couple of students have pointed out

to me that it takes two to tango—the women who got involved with their male teachers were probably seductive. Maybe so, but this simply reflects the fact that they were not yet mature in their practice, and that they were carried away by their investment. The teacher is one who can acknowledge sexual attraction in a dokusan situation, and draw the line at that moment. His role has been entrusted to him by all the Buddhas who have gone before.

However, my critics are correct in the dimension of the larger law—you are responsible for what you do. Not only is the teacher responsible for maintaining a sound relationship with students, and students with their teacher, everybody is responsible for the possible consequences of sexual intercourse. This leads me to abortion again, an example that illustrates the link between the precepts.

In discussing abortion in connection with killing, I began with the pregnant woman in a dilemma. At that point the milk is spilt, and there is no going back to prevent it. But what about before it is spilt? In my view we must acknowledge that sex and fertility cannot be dissociated, whatever mechanical means we may use as birth control. Unwanted pregnancy is a painful reminder of biologically determined nature at work in our bodies; karma that cannot be evaded. Avoiding the problem of abortion begins with a responsible attitude toward sex in the home, including a clear presentation of sexual ethics and their rationale to children when they are growing up.

Sexual ethics is bound up irrevocably with sexual safety. The distinguished husband takes off his three-piece suit. The beautiful wife takes off her makeup. Each trusts the other for the intimate, ancient dance. Mutually taking refuge in this way brings liberation that is fully secure.

But the couple cannot create this protection by themselves. Dante relates how Paolo and Francesca persuaded each other that ideals of true love alone could justify their affair, and they carried this conviction into the Inferno. True partnership is freedom within a publicly expressed commitment, and of such expressions, marriage provides the safest environment. Without marriage, there still can be an agreement to establish a relationship and to work on it. Many people have been harmed by ill-advised marriages, or know others who have been harmed, and so shy away from an ultimate kind of commitment that has a religious foundation and would be hard to break. They form relationships, often successfully, but the lack of ultimate commitment is always a factor, and may prove to be the opening that permits a decision to separate when the relationship becomes difficult.

Commitment in a relationship is the agreement to establish a practice of marriage together. The couple reaches a mutual understanding: "It is not so much that we agree to love and honor each other, though that is an important part of it, but that we agree to love and honor our practice of marriage . We are two people involved in creating a work of art together."

In marriage, man and woman cultivate a harmony with their vastly different psyches, each completing the other, each finding the other in the self, the self in the other, the yin and yang of the universe at play in a single household. Consenting to any sexual affair will involve this dynamism of male and female to some degree. If the intention is directed toward establishing a practice, then the game can move toward liberation. But if other spouses and children are left behind, then the affair can be the source of acute misery. And if deception is involved, then the lives of those concerned are poisoned, and Zen practice, if any, is out the window. Depending on character and circumstances, all

this suffering either cannot be healed, or it can be the whetstone for bringing new life.

The practice of marriage is the lifetime cultivation of intimacy with an opposite. My father used to call my mother "Mrs. Me." Aside from the overtones of male superiority (she did not call him "Mr. Me"), you can sense that he knew how he and his wife were a union. Such union is realized more and more deeply as the years pass, and when one partner ultimately dies, the other lives on for a while assured that the two are still one.

Very different is the argument that sex is fulfilling only when it breaks the established pattern—that human beings are not essentially monogamous. This is the view of people who cultivate power to attract others rather than a compassionate spirit in reaching out to them. Saving all beings is our practice, and in the home this can be just the simple act of doing the dishes or helping with homework— or it can be having a party when the kids are in bed. The dance of sex, the dance of life in all circumstances requires forgetting the self and giving over to the dance. Sexual intercourse is the dancing nucleus of our home, generating all beings at climax, bringing rest and renewal.

We reveal to ourselves the vanity of fulfillment as a goal when we daydream about sex. How much time have you wasted in the arms of your lover, perhaps a true lover of the past, perhaps a lover that never was, while you sit there on your cushions, your back bent slightly forward at your waistline, your eyelids two-thirds lowered, immobile as a stone Buddha, in mock zazen? How much time have you wasted as a Zendo resident, fooling around in sexual games?

The Three Wheels are pure—can you realize this? As the Buddha said, we cannot testify to such facts because of our delusions and attachments. It is time to see through those empty clouds and into the source, once and for all. There is no misuse of sex at the source, no need to prove anything, no boorish self-centeredness at all.

CHAPTER FIVE

The Fourth
Grave Precept

Not Lying

The Chinese ideographs *wang-yü* (Japanese: *mōgo*) are found in combination in the title of the Fourth Precept, and not commonly elsewhere. The etymological meaning is "forgetful or neglectful words." Deriving from this root meaning, the Buddhist and secular dictionaries offer: "a lie, a deliberate lie, wild statements, to tell a lie." Nakagawa Sōen Roshi used to paraphrase Dogen Zenji, saying, "Don't use rootless words."[1]

Thus we are cautioned to be loyal to the essence, and not so much to be true to others. The by-product of such loyalty is that we *are* true to others, but the inspiration is Buddha-nature.

When this is clear, then the various social and psychological virtues of truth-telling are illumined. Self-deception, deception of others, cheating, gossip, and carelessness with language are all disloyal to the peace in our heart of hearts. Words expressive of that peace are true. Silence expressive of that peace is true.

The peace of the vast and fathomless void, full of possibilities, is set forth clearly in the words of our ancestor:

49

Bodhidharma said, "Self-nature is subtle and mysterious. In the realm of the inexplicable Dharma, not preaching a single word is called the Precept of Not Lying."

The phrase "not preaching a single word" is open to misunderstanding, but the Buddha himself turned the wheel of the Dharma in total silence when a philosopher said to him, "I do not ask for words; I do not ask for nonwords." The Buddha just sat there, and the philosopher's delusions vanished like clouds before a strong wind.[2]

In Western culture, we have a long tradition for silence as a presentation of the truth, beginning with Jesus as he stood before Pilate, and continuing to the present day in American courts of law, where "standing mute" is one option open to the defendant when asked, "Guilty or not guilty?" The *Cheng-tao ko* says:

> It speaks in silence;
> in speech you hear its silence.[3]

When we can't hear the silence in the words of others, we know something is wrong. But it is not easy to notice the error in ourselves. Hamlet sought to catch the conscience of the Queen, and she remarked of herself projected on stage, "The lady doth protest too much, methinks,"[4] not fully realizing that the play related to her. Most of the rest of us need a strong reminder too, one way or another.

But the truth is there, even in mindless chatter. I used to marvel at how my old teachers would nod and beam as their students babbled on and on.

Dogen Zenji said, "The Dharma wheel turns from the beginning. There is neither surplus nor lack. The whole universe is moistened with nectar, and the truth is ready to harvest."

Not only is the truth already there, it is altogether delightful and ready to be accepted. Take me, says the fact. Feng-hsüeh presented such a fact to a monk who was also concerned about words and nonwords:

"Speech is a matter of subject and object. Silence is a matter of subject and object. How may I be free of subject and object?"

Feng-hsueh said, "I always think of Chiang-nan in March. Partridges chirp among the many fragrant flowers."[5]

Feng-hsueh and the Buddha used compassionate, expedient means to present the truth incisively. At other times in their lives, their actions and words were truthful, but directed to quite ordinary purposes, such as asking for water or accepting a gift. Our own lives are full of ordinary purposes, and also of crises. How may we be expressive of the truth in dealing with them?

The doctor often faces the question of whether or not to tell a patient that an illness is terminal. I recall speaking with someone from Japan who was giving me news of our friends there. He mentioned a person we both knew well and said he had undergone an operation for cancer.

"Of course he doesn't know," my friend said. "He thinks it is just an ulcer." This reflects a Japanese cultural interpretation of the Fourth Precept. There it is widely assumed that it is not compassionate to tell sick people the hard truth about their terminal illness. In our culture, we are starting to believe that it is important to tell patients the objective fact and to help them become reconciled to it. We are learning from social research that they really know anyway, and we are coming to feel that we should not encourage false games at the very time when sick people and their families can realize the deepest dimensions of their relationship.

What kind of karma does deception about the fatal illness set up for the dying person? I don't know, but I sense that it is dreadful. Perhaps this is how ghosts are born. And if the family members are at all sensitive, the effect will be felt as unfinished business that cannot be finished.

We generate ghosts in ordinary times too, leaving communications unfinished, conveying mistaken impressions, failing to share. The "Net of Indra" inspires me to regard the universe as a great communications workshop, in which you and I practice the expression of compassionate truth with all beings, and encourage that practice in others toward ourselves.

"Not Lying" has its application in Right Livelihood and Right Lifestyle, and may involve Right Social Activism. Not only must I not work for an ordinary advertising agency, but I must not swallow advertising lies either. Not lying means no complicity with lies. One of my students wrote to me, "One of my strongest reasons for not registering for the draft and then resisting it publicly was my wish to resist the lies of power."

There are, however, niches in our mendacious society for the truthseeker. There is "honest business"; there are even unusual advertising agencies. Depending upon personal character and a variety of other factors (including the responsibility to help feed a family), one can elect to stay on the corporate bus and try to influence its direction, or get off and walk. Right Livelihood is not solely a literal injunction, but also a matter of responding wisely to circumstances.

This wisdom arises from innate honesty. Ethics is common sense—the sense we have in common. When a parent declares that a six-year-old child is only five in order to avoid paying an extra fare, the child learns dishonesty. If the parent acknowledges the child's correct age and buys the extra ticket, then the inherent honesty of the child is confirmed. "I'm six years old"—that's the truth.

In Japan, the Zen student is exhorted to be "sincere." I prefer the word "honest." Though your work is focusing on Mu, many tempting thoughts wait in the wings. With just a moment's inattention, they come pouring forth. Be honest and stay attentive. Be in touch with your innate honesty, and your zazen will be the foundation of an honest life.

This honesty is also creative. Manner and content, the two criteria of an appropriate response in the dokusan room, both come from integrity. With regard to manner, one thing that strikes us in Chinese Zen dialogues, even in their translated form, is vividness of language. We say their words are poetry, but what is poetry, or prose for that matter, but faithfulness to language? Sloppy language is a kind of disloyalty to humanity, a kind of lying. Talent for language is one of the few qualities that distinguishes human beings from other animals, but this talent is often dulled by the abstract discipline of some kinds of education, and one finds relatively illiterate people who are more closely in touch with language (and thus with themselves) than professors of philosophy. I recall discussing the roads of Eastern Oregon with a woodsman there, who complained that he had to replace his tires much more often now that his son had a girl friend. "I tell you," he said, "dancin' is very hard on tires." In touch with ourselves, we speak faithfully.

The content of the response is just as revealing as the manner. Deeper than culture, transcending expedience, beyond morality, the great truth cannot be concealed:

> At the end of the summer training period, Ts'ui-yen said to his assembly, "All summer I have been preaching to you brothers. Look closely, do I still have my eyebrows?"[6]

It is said that when a Zen teacher preaches false dharma (the worst kind of lying) his eyebrows fall off. But Ts'ui-yen is revealing everything, to the very bottom. Yüan-wu says that of all the ancients, Ts'ui-yen is one of the greatest:

> Many people misunderstand and say, "Under the bright sun in the blue sky, Ts'ui-yen spoke aimless talk producing concern where there was none; at the end of the summer he spoke of his own faults and examined them himself first to avoid others criticizing him." Fortunately this has nothing to do with it. Such views are called the exterminators of the Buddha race.[7]

"Look at the way he talks," Yuan-wu challenges us. "What is his true meaning?"[8] Don't be fooled. There is no "meaning" here at all. There is no sword hidden in Ts'ui-yen's words. The truth is ready to harvest. Interpretation, disguised as meaning, gets in the way of truth, all too often.

I remember cringing at the words of Charles Manson and his followers during their trials for murder. For them, it seems, killing was the way to prove the truth of oneness. Even murder, they seemed to say, is no different from making love. The truth is ready to harvest, but you must be ready to harvest it. The nature of oneness is emptiness, full of unique possibilities. Interpreting oneness just in the dimension of possibilities, that is, in the phenomenal dimension, led to a terrible tragedy.

The Manson case is an example of metaphysical perversity, but ordinary lies bring disorganization and suffering to families, communities, nations, and the world. The Three Poisons of self-centered motivation destroy our consciousness of the interrelationship of all beings, and give rise to poisonous responses all around.

Practicing truth, on the other hand, is practice in community organization. Several years ago we experimented with Gestalt therapy at the Maui Zendo, turning ourselves into a "group" once a week for three hours, under the leadership of a skilled facilitator. It was difficult to switch from focusing on Mu to acting out dreams and childhood memories, and back, but it has proved to be worthwhile, for that summer of group therapy laid the groundwork for the sharing meetings we have held since at the Diamond Sangha centers—sangha experiments with truth.

We gather periodically, sometimes just the residents of the center, sometimes the entire sangha, and share our thoughts and feelings on a particular theme, always with a leader to keep us from talking out of turn or getting too abstract. At our meeting on abortion, the women felt safe enough to share their intimate experiences, and their feelings and thoughts about them. Several women found themselves released from their deep sorrows at last, and the men, including me, learned more deeply what it is to be female. As men and women together in these meetings, we learn to be intimate with ourselves and each other through the practice of truth.

Truth, like sex, needs a safe environment. If I speak from my heart, I want to feel that you are listening. The truth is ready to be harvested, but it cannot be heard if "I am here and you are out there." We have such bad habits of not listening and not telling the truth that one psychologist I know has developed workshops devoted to learning how to pay attention to what people say, and how to speak clearly and honestly.

The risk is that sharing can become license for "dumping"—I feel much better on relieving my mind of its poisonous burden, but everybody else feels much worse. This is not communication, but projection. Hostility is reinforced and the poisons are intensified. However, when a culture of honesty develops in the family or sangha, dumping is transformed to an unselfish act of opening the heart, and the Net of Indra is realized.

Psychological practice of openness to the other person goes hand in hand with the Zen practice of openness to all beings—to the doves in the avocado tree, to the stones in the garden, to the sun, the moon, and the stars. This is none other than *daigo*, great enlightenment, "the daily activity of the Buddhas, but they never think about it."[9] Don't be carried away by your smooth talk. I too must be careful about this.

The Fourth Precept, like all the others, finds its home in zazen, in the vast and fathomless void. It also finds its home in family conferences, in business meetings, and in dealing privately with personal inadequacies. The truth expressed with love is the sangha treasure, moistened with nectar.

CHAPTER SIX

The Fifth
Grave Precept

*Not Giving
or Taking Drugs*

> Shakyamuni Buddha said, "Now when I view all beings everywhere, I see that each of them possesses the wisdom and virtue of the *Tathāgata*, but because of their attachments and delusions, they cannot bear witness to that fact."[1]

Tathagata is another name for Buddha—literally, "the one who just comes." The one who comes forth purely from essential nature, as essential nature.

All precepts reiterate the Buddha's words. In this case, one can say, all beings of the universe are unclouded from the beginning, but the haze created by their use of drink and drugs keeps them from acknowledging it.

There are many ways to cloud the mind, and this precept encompasses them all. Following it literally would mean not drinking alcohol or smoking grass at all. I think it is possible to move graciously through the world without taking a social drink, or accepting a hit as the marijuana cigarette makes its rounds. For myself I simply say I don't care for the way it affects me, when it is necessary to offer any explanation at all. In fact, if I am going to do zazen soon, even half a glass of beer will affect my practice adversely. It will also affect my judgment in any situation away from my cushions, and I will not be as clear-minded as I might be otherwise.

The person who becomes intoxicated habitually is harming the body, and the body is none other than the dojo of the Buddha. It takes a long time to flush out the residue of all that poison. Moreover, the frequent use of marijuana (or stronger drugs) sets up a pattern of avoiding the low emotional places in life. This is a false path, for eventually drug use brings one to even lower places. The best therapy is the practice of acknowledging one's feelings and making friends with them. Then they can be seen as truly transparent.

Not selling drink or drugs is likewise a matter of personal practice, but we cannot be "holier than thou." Our society is structured on the Three Poisons of greed, hatred, and ignorance. Probably selling drink or drugs is no worse than selling cars, which destroy many lives, make highways necessary, and reinforce the oil mania. Pushing heroin spiked with rat poison on a street corner is hardly Right Livelihood, but it is paradigmatic of corporations dumping carcinogenic insecticides on Latin American peasants.

We are enmeshed in this cruel, acquisitive system. The tricycle your child rides may very well have been manufactured by Seagram's Distilleries, or worse. When we acknowledge our own membership in the corporation, we can "speak truth to power" effectively from the boardroom itself.

Currently, the sale of marijuana and other drugs is illegal in the United States and most other countries. This adds another dimension to the precept, for traffic in such drugs places one in a paranoid state of mind. Paranoia is the ultimate distraction, but it is also perversely expressive of the truth: we are not separate from others. The peace we seek in our Zen practice will be very elusive if we are always on the lookout for informers, mistrusting even our sisters and brothers.

If one is casual toward marijuana laws, perhaps this reflects a casual attitude toward secular laws generally, for example, those relating to crosswalks or building permits. If the law of the land is unjust, as it is in repressive countries, then the truth seeker speaks out, or goes underground to speak out another day. But even in a relatively enlightened society, a particular statute may violate the law we know in our hearts. Then surely it is our responsibility to say it is wrong, and perhaps even to violate it openly as a means of public education—or else avoid the circumstances completely. Practice is not limited to the cushions in the dojo.

Right Livelihood and Right Lifestyle are Right Practice, and are inadvertently teaching. In his poem attached to Case 37 of the *Wu-men kuan*, Chao-chou's "Oak Tree in the Garden," Wu-men wrote: "Speech is not an expedient":

> A monk asked Chao-chou, "What is the reason Bodhidharma came from the west?"
> Chao-chou said, "Oak tree in the garden." [2]

Chao-chou did not say "Oak tree in the garden" for the purpose of enlightening the monk before him. But it did, or we presume so. Likewise, if my polite refusal of a drink is simply that, and not intended to influence others, still it inevitably does, whether or not I am a professional teacher. The same is true for Right Livelihood. The purpose is personal practice, but others will inevitably be affected.

This is not to say that you cannot learn from a drunk. You can, and not merely by negative example. A Zen teacher who drinks excessively or gets stoned on grass can still be a teacher. However, the students of such teachers are placed in the awkward position of acknowledging their teacher's apparent violation of precepts while accepting his or her guidance in other aspects of the practice. I have heard it said of a certain Buddhist teacher that his heavy indulgences are a high teaching of nonattachment even to the precepts. This is an ethical gyration that could be used to justify the entire spectrum of criminal behavior.

There have been prominent Buddhist figures who have enjoyed wine. One thinks of Ikkyū Zenji, the monk Ryō-kan, and, in our own times, Yamamoto Gempo Roshi. Ik-kyu for one was imprecise in following other precepts and such imperfection must be weighed with his admirable qualities and achievements.

The first time I met Gempo Roshi, he was already in his middle eighties. It was winter, and he sat bundled against the cold he felt keenly in his old age, sipping sake, and munching toasted *mochi*. He exuded warmth and love and was a great teacher for a young Westerner uptight with as-cetic preoccupations.

In Psalm 104, David gives thanks to the Lord for his gift of wine "that maketh glad the heart of man," and the place of wine as the blood of the Redeemer in Christian ceremony gives it a central role in Christian faith. One must also weigh the medicinal qualities of alcohol and marijuana, and their social value. If liquor and marijuana impair the judgment, they also help people to overcome their isolation from each other. As a Zen teacher, I know very well that drugs have opened the door to religious possibilities for many people.

All this ambiguity prompts one to seek the ground of the precept:

> Bodhidharma said "Self-nature is subtle and mysterious. In the realm of the intrinsically pure Dharma, not giving rise to delusions is called the Precept of Not Giving or Taking Drugs."

As always, Bodhidharma hews to the severe line of the unconditioned absolute. By this I do not, of course, mean that he insists upon a literal moral position, but that he points to essential nature. Why can't the rest of us testify to such nature? It is not only drink, or drugs, or tobacco, or coffee, or TV, or whatever. What is happening in your mind? Do you provide your own barbituates? All of us do, and so all of us violate this precept.

It is really the Three Poisons that this precept is about, self-centered delusions that cloud and darken the mind in our world of Zen practice, and in our application of realization in our everyday life. Victimized by our own separation from others, we drink to break down inhibitions. But when we dwell in that place where every day is truly a good day, a little wine, or the Chinese thrush, or meeting an old friend from far away, can gladden our hearts.

> Dogen Zenji said, "Drugs are not brought in yet. Don't let them invade. That is the great light."

I am reminded of our teacher Katsuki Sekida's admonitions about zazen. Sometimes he would prompt us throughout an entire period of sitting, saying "Don't let them invade!" or words to that effect.

> When Chao-chou was sweeping the courtyard, a monk asked, "How can a speck of dust come into this holy ground?"
> Chao-chou said, "Here comes another!"[3]

Chao-chou and Dogen are not saying that the absence of thoughts is *ipso-facto* the great light. A blank mind is likely to be quite dull. Yet that dull state is, in the practice of zazen, the temporary condition of stuckness, to use Robert Pirsig's term. It is not a condition of separation, and if we reach out from it we find only darkness:

Yun-men said to his assembly, "Each of you has your own light. If you want to see it, you cannot. The darkness is dark, dark. Now, what is your light?"

Answering for his listeners, he said, "The storeroom, the gate!" [4]

Light is the ten thousand things advancing and confirming the self: the Chinese thrush, the gate, a sip of wine. How else may we take our pleasure here?

Our channels of habitual thinking are deeply cut, and the links of association are tight and almost inevitable. When the gecko calls, do you think about the gecko? Do you think about the geckos at your house? Here comes another call! Sparks to light your Dharma candle go off one after another. The storeroom, the gate!

Thus things of the world are not drugs in themselves. They become drugs by our use of them. We direct all phenomena to justify ourselves, and that, as Dogen Zenji said, is delusion. [5] But such fine words butter no parsnips. How can we avoid self-centeredness? How can we prevent *them* from invading? Shaku Sōen Zenji said, "When you go to sleep, sleep as if you were entering your last sleep. When you awaken, leave your bed behind immediately, as though casting away an old pair of shoes." [6] In those moments before you go to sleep, and after you awaken before rising, you are vulnerable to drugs of the mind. (The chemicals drugs produce in the brain already exist there in small amounts.) At the same time, the moment between sleeping and waking, or waking and sleeping, may be the *nen* of realization, as some of our sangha members have discovered.

What is a good way to enter your last sleep? With an empty mind, surely—the mind of infinite peace. Breathing Mu is my favorite way of going to sleep. At first I am just breathing Mu, inhale and exhale, settling down. At last I enter the silence of Mu, and my dream companions gather. Somehow I practice Mu with them, it seems.

What is a good way to awaken? Is Mu your first thought? Make it your second, at least, and soon enough it will be your first. On your cushions, each breath is a going to sleep; each breath a wakening. With each exhalation, leave everything behind, except your practice. In daily life, your practice will be your task at hand and your movement from one thing to another, including, of course, recreation and rest. But wherever you are, self-centered thoughts are waiting in the wings. Give them a wave, but don't let them take over. This is the enlightenment of all the Buddhas, the precept of not taking drink or drugs.

CHAPTER SEVEN

The Sixth
Grave Precept
Not Discussing
Faults of Others

> If you do not pass the barrier of the founding teachers, if you
> do not cut off the mind road, then you are like a ghost,
> clinging to bushes and grasses.
>
> *Wu-men kuan*, Case 1[1]

This passage is familiar to Zen students. At least in the Diamond Sangha they hear it in the course of every sesshin. The
barrier is the koan Mu, and the mind road is the endless
stream of words and images in our heads.

To cut off the mind road is to experience total silence, so
that circumstances can be seen clearly and taken in cleanly,
each one fresh and new. Not to cut it off is to continue
projecting one's own confused images on the world and
then to cling to them.

Wu-men's teisho on Case 1 of his *Wu-men kuan* deals pri-
marily with passing the barrier. The Sixth Precept empha-
sizes cutting off the mind road. The two lessons clarify each
other. The realized mind is at rest, and deals with things as
they are; the ghost mind is noisy and deals with its own
creations.

Bodhidharma said, "Self-nature is subtle and mysterious. In the realm of the flawless Dharma, not expounding upon error is called the Precept of Not Speaking of Faults of Others."

These words may seem a denial of the everyday world where some people are weak and other people are irritable. But the Dharma and everyday life are the same. One person is indeed strong; another is indeed weak. One person is serene; another irritable. The way of the Sixth Precept is the way of Jesus when he said, "Judge not, that you be not judged." [2] From Bodhidharma's point of view, this would mean, "When you judge, you place yourself in the dimension of good and bad." Or, as Wu-men wrote, "If you argue right and wrong, you are a person of right and wrong." [3]

The mind that is not relative is silent. With a truly silent mind, the self is forgotten, and the myriad things are our own essential nature. This is not a relatively quiet condition, but the peace that passes all understanding. Forgetting the self is not a matter of getting rid of the self; in fact, realization is a matter of seeing yourself more clearly. What do you see? As the Bodhisattva Avalokiteshvara tells you when you recite the *Heart Sutra*, all those things that bind you together are empty. [4] There is nothing to hold on to at all, and so you are free to give your attention to what is happening in the ephemeral world.

The ephemeral world is made up of relative elements, high and low, light and dark, loud and quiet. The Sixth Precept shows us how we can find intimacy with this world. The silent mind intuits directly and truly, "She has an awful temper," or, "He is thoughtless of his friends." These can be experienced as basic information, free of any moral judgment and on a par with "Her hair is brown" or "He has big feet." On the other hand, fault-finding, discussing the faults of others—these are acts of rejection. The difference is one of attitude.

> Dogen Zenji said, "In the Buddha Dharma, there is one path, one Dharma, one realization, one practice. Don't permit fault-finding. Don't permit haphazard talk."

While Bodhidharma points to essence, Dogen Zenji shows us the way to practice it. He insists again that we must be single-minded. Reject everything except the Buddha Tao! Among the things we must reject are fault-finding and haphazard speech.

The fabric of the Buddha sangha is as fragile as the intention of a single member. One person can create havoc in the group by malicious talk. In the original Japanese, the word Yamada Roshi and I translated as "haphazard" can also mean "causing disorder, causing laxity, causing demoralization."

I suggest that you and I be careful in following Dogen Zenji's caution. Almost all of us respond immaturely to others and cling to the bushes and grasses we have created. We say, "He is a woman-chaser; she is lazy; that other person is aloof," and we react to these people accordingly. We distrust the woman-chaser; we avoid giving the lazy one an important task; and we turn our own resentment and aloofness onto the withdrawn person.

In the Sarvodaya Movement of village self-reliance in Sri Lanka, participants are encouraged to practice "sharing language," *priyavachana* (pleasant or kindly speech) as one of the principles of social behavior. People of all ranks and backgrounds are addressed as "older sister," "younger brother," "mother," and so on. Priyavachana is also taken to mean that Sarvodayans "speak to each other in mutually

supportive ways, avoiding . . . malicious gossip."⁵ This
practice is rooted in the ancient Buddhist doctrine of Right
Speech and is the way of any religion worthy of the name. It
is a matter of checking the internal chatter and practicing
compassion.

There are many things in the sangha that need correct-
ing. Many things need reordering. But such corrections
can be made without finding faults and without being haphazard and destructive. When I hear people condemn a fellow student in our sangha, I acknowledge my own faults,
my own inadequacy as a teacher, for my students have not
yet touched the place where there are no faults, and are not,
in the instance at hand, practicing to reach that place. I acknowledge that our dojo is not a dojo. Let's remember our
purpose!

It is not easy. Just as we practice Mu when it is not clear,
so we practice intimacy when we do not feel it. Just as we
return again and again to Mu after drifting into remember-
ing and planning, so we return again and again to intimacy
when we drift into discussing the faults of others. How
should you return? Like zazen, it is a matter of practice.
When you notice, or when someone brings your aloofness
to your attention, directly or indirectly, take the appropriate steps to restore your intimacy.

I remember a particular instance of aloofness by the entire sangha at the Maui Zendo. One of our members was, we
agreed, a woman-chaser. His nickname was "Lover-boy."
The women avoided him completely or played his sexual
games. The men did no better and seemed governed by
their attitude toward his reputation. None of us could look
him in the eye and deal with him as a person.

Such a "problem" does not belong to a single individual.
When we labeled our brother "Lover-boy," we conspired to

isolate him. Collectively we washed our hands of him. Our failure as a sangha resulted in his departure from the Zendo.

If the sangha is able to respond without labeling, however, the success may be startling. One of our present members at the Maui Zendo works hard at a demanding job. Old-timers remember how he appeared, just out of school, with no work experience and no inclination to lift dishcloth to dish. Any business would have fired him within a week. But the Zendo is not a business, and we were able to devote ourselves to him. When we gave him important tasks without projecting any concept of laziness onto him, he found that he was being treated like anybody else, and given equal responsibility. We appealed to his better nature out of our own better nature, and he responded at that level, rather than by his old habit. This did not happen the first time or the second, but today he is a different person.

Somehow we were able to deal better with the issue of work than with the issue of sex, but both examples are instructive. Trust and intimacy are the *upāya*, appropriate means. When they are present in our group, we ourselves are the Buddha's dojo. Then there are no outsiders to put into boxes. We include people, animals, trees, stones, and clouds by our realization of Buddha-nature: the other is no other than myself. In Mahayana terms, when I forget the self, I find that the other is nurturing me. In fact, realization of Buddha-nature is not possible alone, and not possible unless one is open to nurturing. Give the other a chance. Do you say this is naive? Maybe so, but look where sophistication has brought us.

The problem is that we get hooked by appearances and are no longer standing on our own feet. With trust, however, we can pay attention to the innate person out there. If someone is aloof, perhaps a smile and a friendly question, or perhaps simply respectful silence may be appropriate. The question is, who is boss here? Are you blown about by the words and actions of others, or do you sit firmly in your own dojo of intimacy? When something happens, do you use that chance, or are you used by it?

You have a role as "other," of course, and at the appropriate occasion your act of nurturing will enhance the dojo of a friend. Here is Ben Franklin being nurtured:

> My list of virtues contain'd at first but twelve; but a Quaker friend having kindly informed me that I was generally thought proud, that my pride show'd itself frequently in conversation; that I was not content with being in the right when discussing any point, but was overbearing and rather insolent, of which he convinc'd me by mentioning several instances; I determined endeavoring to cure myself, if I could, of this vice or folly among the rest, and I added *Humility* to my list.[6]

Thus it is possible for you to perceive my faults and remain clear and compassionate—to perceive even the faults of publicans and sinners, heroin dealers, pimps, and arms manufacturers, and not be knocked off balance.

Actually, a so-called fault is a weak place where character can change. Your quality of stubbornness, your quality of passivity, your quality of anger—these are the sensitive places in your personality where your individual talent can emerge. It is your anger that will enable you to correct evil in the world. It is your stubbornness that will enable you to realize Mu. It is your passivity that will enable you to endure hardship on the path. When you truly see how much change can occur in yourself and how you can use your qualities of character, then you will appreciate how others may do so also.

Holding on to old perceptions of each other keeps members of any community aloof from each other, and this is particularly noticeable in the Buddha sangha. I was once a member of a small sangha where certain people were not speaking to certain other people, all because of incidents that had taken place twenty-five years earlier. When you let go of your old perceptions, you give people a chance to change. When you do not let go, you are participating in the continuation of their faults.

My teacher, Yasutani Haku'un Roshi, had a hot temper. Looking at his life story, I can see how this anger must have been built into his psyche from earliest childhood. We can be sure that in his youth it caused him suffering, but as a Zen teacher he channeled this passion most effectively. He felt betrayed by the Soto Zen hierarchy which could not provide a teacher to guide him. After he found Harada Dai'un Roshi, he broke away from the Soto Zen structure and founded his own Dharma path. He never stopped pointing out specific errors of contemporary priests, and his fierce words awakened many people to their own errors.

People would ask him, "Aren't you violating the Sixth Precept by talking about the Soto hierarchy in this way?" He would reply, "We must correct mistaken and haphazard Dharma teaching. . . . If we neglect to do this, we are violating the precept."[7]

The Roshi used his passion to uphold the Dharma, saying, in effect, "I am pointing to specific errors in the most appropriate manner I can. This is not 'discussing faults of others,' but indeed, it is fulfilling the intention of all the precepts—to clarify the Buddha Tao."

Sometimes it may be necessary and appropriate for me to say to someone in confidence, "I am not sure that you can get the best kind of training at such-and-such place, or with such-and-such a teacher." Not to do so would be to violate the principle of all precepts. But if you ask me in open meeting what I think of Doodad Roshi, I am likely to make a vague response. Is your purpose to establish a concept of someone's character, or is it to find guidance?

Like Frankenstein, we create monsters with words, and while our creations have no fundamental validity, they fix images in the minds of all, including those whom we gossip about. Even when we can support our condemnation with data, we may be preventing growth. With growth, insincerity becomes true love. With growth, conceit becomes leadership. But if negative qualities are fixed in everybody's heads, growth is made very difficult.

The distinction between appropriate identification of weaknesses and fault-finding may be seen in comparing dokusan work with random gossip. When you say, "My concentration is getting better," I may say, "So long as you are concentrating on Mu, there are two things. You are still separate from Mu. Let Mu breathe Mu." I think you can appreciate the specific nature of this response. I am not establishing a fixed concept of your character.

What is the outcome of appropriate identification? This is, after all, a question pointing to the outcome of all precepts, the response of people to the guidance implicit in right words and right actions.

Mu-chou asked a monk, "Where have you just come from?"
The monk shouted.
Mu-chou said, "That's a shout on me."
The monk shouted again.
Mu-chou said, "Three shouts, four shouts, what then?"
The monk said nothing.
Mu-chou hit him and said, "You thieving phoney!"[8]

When Mu-chou said, "That's a shout on me," he was saying, rather ironically, "You got one up on me in this Dharma combat." But the monk did not notice any irony, and went on to repeat himself. The final hit and invective formed Mu-chou's ultimate effort to bring the monk around, every bit as compassionate as the words of Ben Franklin's friend. The difference is that a realization of essential nature was at stake here, not merely awareness of moral weakness.

When people replied inadequately to Jesus on one occasion, he said, "Verily, I say to you that the publicans and harlots go into the Kingdom of God before you."[9] That was a great scolding! Surely some of his listeners got the point.

Getting the point is the outcome of scolding when the mind is ripened and the occasion is appropriate, whether the scolding comes from outside or whether it is self-induced. At a psychological level, a generalization such as "I feel worthless" or "I am threatened by women" can be a truth, reached by much inner difficulty, that is liberating. It will be a provisional truth, for there is another step to self-worth and confidence, but until you can acknowledge your weaknesses and attachments, it is impossible to let go of them. Helping another on this path is a way to fulfill the Sixth Precept.

There is, however, an even deeper liberation that is far more than just finding confidence. Hsüeh-tou included a passage from the *Diamond Sutra* in his *Blue Cliff Record* in order to clarify this deepest release:

> If you are despised by others and are about to fall into hell because of your evil karma in your previous life, then because you are despised by others the evil karma of your previous life will be extinguished.[10]

"You thieving phoney!" Mu-chou is not merely making a precise description of a fault. Everything disappears at that point, and the Sixth Precept is fulfilled.

CHAPTER EIGHT

The Seventh
Grave Precept

Not Praising Yourself
While Abusing Others

> As one who truly practices the Tao,
> Don't regard the world as ignorant.
> If you condemn the world,
> That is your own condemnation.
>
> *The Platform Sutra* [1]

I remember when I got my first koan from Senzaki Sensei. I went around looking at other people, thinking how special I was. It was quite an innocent attitude, I think, for I was feeling sorry that other people could not have a koan too, but it could easily have become arrogance. Arrogance condemns the arrogant one, as Hui-neng says. It announces to the world that I do not feel at ease with myself, and so I must summon up self-praise, and go about abusing other people.

Examples of self-condemnatory arrogance are all about us. Look at the foreign policy of the United States: it is clear that abuse of other nations and praise of our own is a product of national defensiveness and fear. We doubt our own worth and feel vulnerable, so we lash out to prevent others from attacking us first. Of course the United States is not alone in such behavior; we see the same foreign policy in the actions of other countries, and of smaller groups too, not to mention individuals.

Put arrogance to rest. Begin with zazen, and let everything else go, focus only on Mu, and become Mu. Then in daily life also, focus on the sangha task, and let everything else go.

When your child spills her milk, you have a number of options for a response. The karma of the situation inevitably will include many factors, so the best response cannot be set forth abstractly. It might be direct correction. It might be simply, "Oh, let's clean it up." The key point is that if your mind is at rest, you are free to be a wise parent, to speak and act in keeping with the Tao, and to teach the Tao with your speech and action.

But when your mind is not at rest you are not steadfast, and you look for defenses. It is the other person who is no good. Then you say, "You are always spilling your milk," while you yourself are beyond error—the unassailable parent.

Hui-neng says:

> Even with a steadfast body you may be deluded and speak of the bad qualities of others as soon as you open your mouth, and thus behave in opposition to the Tao.[2]

Make no mistake. Hui-neng uses strong language, but opposition to the realization of another and of oneself is not any kind of original sin. It is rather a clouding of the fact that all beings are the Tathagata. "Point to the Tao of the Buddha," Hui-neng is saying, "and let your mind be at ease."

When Te-shan's student Hsüeh-feng reproved him for coming to dinner before the bell rang, Te-shan simply turned around and went back to his room.[3] The meal was late, but Te-shan did not justify his own action or criticize

Hsueh-feng. He did not say, even gently, "You know, we have only so much time for dinner. When the meal is late, rest-time is cut short for the monks. Our schedule is tight in this monastery; and when rest-time is cut short, the monks have no way to catch up." No, he was totally at ease and serene—able to take correction and teach in return.

Turning around was Te-shan's perfect presentation of the whole matter, but Hsueh-feng didn't get it, and went on to justify himself to Yen-t'ou. He felt proud that he had defeated his old teacher, and didn't notice that he had been given a lesson. Sometimes even when the mother will say, "Oh, let's clean it up," the child will respond, "I didn't mean to spill it!" instead of going after the sponge. We can't expect our sensitive response to be successful in each instance, at least not in the short term. Te-shan seemed to fail for the moment, but his action ultimately enlightens us all, because his heart was completely pure.

Te-shan was ready to be taught by his own student, and this is no more than simple modesty. It is acknowledgment of the affinity of all things, openness not only to a seven-year-old child, as in the case of Chao-chou, but to the expectations of your dog. The thrush has something to say to you.

At a sesshin in Kamakura, a senior student laughed loudly during a rest period. Many people would react angrily to such a distraction during sesshin, and might complain to the roshi that such behavior is unworthy of an advanced student. But for one student that loud laugh was the occasion of her *kenshō*. It was the spark that lit her Dharma candle. When self and other, proper and improper, are forgotten, then we find good teaching all around. With such an open spirit, fleas teach us, intestinal worms teach us. Our great mountain Haleakala teaches us. The grass in our compound teaches us.

With delusions of superiority, however, good teaching

goes unnoticed, and the sparks simply go out. With attachments to old neuroses of fear and defense, your readiness is self-centered. What are you ready for? Are you ready for the Chinese thrush? Are you ready for insightful comment? Or are you ready to attack? If you cover over your weaknesses and single out the weaknesses of others, then you are not practicing. It is only when you can generously acknowledge your own dark side and the shining side of the other that you can be said to be truly on the path.

One of my most endearing memories is of a family that I lived with for a while many years ago. The father and mother both had low-paying jobs, and there were many pressures. They worked things out by role-playing each other. The daughter would play her cranky mother; the mother her demanding daughter, each laughing at herself as she saw her precious concerns parodied from outside. The outside plays the inside, as you hear when the owl calls in the early evening.

In the dojo too, the roles are always moving around. Beginners play the leaders. If you are always on time, perform your assigned work carefully, keep well groomed and tidy, and sit diligently, then that is leadership—it encourages others. The inside is open to instruction; the outside is the field of practice.

Always we return to the Middle Way. When you are not self-consciously clever, you can enhance the Dharma. When you are not constitutionally suspicious of motives of others, then true character change and a mind receptive to realization may be possible.

Bodhidharma said, "Self-nature is subtle and mysterious. In the realm of the equitable Dharma, not dwelling upon *I* against *you* is called the Precept of Not Praising Yourself While Abusing Others."

There is no concept of *I* and *you*, no concept of sage and ordinary person, in self-nature. In that place, as Tōrei Enji Zenji said, even a malicious person is the avatar of the Buddha.[4]

> Dogen Zenji said, "Buddhas and Ancestral Teachers realize the empty sky and the great earth. When they manifest the noble body, there is neither inside nor outside in emptiness. When they manifest the Dharma body there is not even a bit of earth on the ground."

How do you put on clothing when there is neither inside nor outside? What remains when there is not a bit of earth on the ground? Other checking questions might be asked about Dogen Zenji's words, but for our purposes we can understand him to mean that truly realized people see clearly the nonduality of *I* and *you*, the emptiness of comparative concepts, and the vanity of a superior manner.

When there is no fixed concept of *I* and *you*, then decision making by a single person is inappropriate. Western Zen centers have inherited rather authoritarian modes of decision making from Japan and Korea, and over the years these have been the cause of distress among members. The roshi acting from the most profound enlightenment can seem high-handed if he or she does not consult adequately with all concerned. In my opinion modes of decision making by consensus, evolved from Quaker models in the Movement for a New Society, offer the Western Zen movement the means to apply the Seventh Precept in their sangha government.[5] The roshi and the sangha are likely to have different interpretations of the Dharma, but through a careful process of sharing, with the roshi taking part, consensus can be found—a creative learning experience all around.

Several years ago, Gary Snyder issued a little broadside, quoting the *Digha Nikaya II*, which provides a certain precedent for consensus decision making in Buddhist tradition. It is worth quoting in full because its references to the respectful treatment of women and to traditional cultural values are also very interesting:

SHAKYAMUNI BUDDHA'S THOUGHTS
ON A RIGHTEOUS SOCIETY

Ajatasattu, King of Magadha, was contemplating attacking the Vajji tribe, but wasn't sure if he could bring it off. He sent a minister to the Buddha, who was camped at Vulture Peak, to ask him what he thought of the Vajji. Shakyamuni and Ananda conferred, and agreed to the following points about the Vajji people:

1. The Vajji people frequently gather together for conference and many people attend such meetings.

2. The Vajji people gather in unison and act in unison to perform necessary tribal undertakings.

3. The Vajji people do not establish rules without precedence nor do they break existing rules, but they live in accord with the traditional laws established in the past.

4. The Vajji people respect, revere, and venerate their elders and consider their advice worthwhile.

5. The Vajji people do not forcefully take and confine girls and women.

6. The Vajji people respect, revere, and venerate their holy places, and do not forego the custom of offerings.

7. The Vajji people provide protection, defense, and support for Arhats, sages, and yogins, hoping that those who have not yet come will enter their territory, and those who reside there will peacefully continue to do so for as long as they may desire.

And the Buddha said, "As long as these seven conditions are observed, the Vajji will prosper, and no decline can take place."[6]

The minister then remarked that if the Vajji observed even one among such conditions, the King of Magadha

would not be able to raise a finger against them. It is said
that the Buddha preached a number of times on these seven
conditions as they applied to his sangha.[7]

Thus the Seventh Precept is a reflex of the First Precept,
"Not Killing." By not praising yourself and abusing others, by using yourself in concert with others to realize the
potential of the biotic community, you are saving all beings. And, as Hui-neng says, saving all beings is saving
them in your own mind.[8] When your mind is one with all
mind, then comparisons are half-truths at best, and your
work is the work of the world.

CHAPTER NINE

The Eighth
Grave Precept

Not Sparing
the Dharma Assets

To review what is meant by "Dharma": It is the essential nature of all things and the universe itself, emptiness that is charged with possibilities. It is the possibilities themselves as they come forth into being and then pass away. It is the interaction of beings, their interpenetration and mutual dependence.

The Dharma is also the special law found in particular doctrines. Buddha Dharma is Buddhist law. It is cosmic law as interpreted by the Buddha and his successors. We say the Buddha turned the Wheel of the Law. That is, he put cosmic Dharma into expression.

Scientific Dharma, if I may use that phrase, is cosmic law interpreted by biologists and physicists. $E = mc^2$ is a description of how things are, and anyone who tries to evade it will be frustrated. The same is true of the Buddha Dharma; it cannot be ignored.

When Pai-chang gave a certain series of talks, an old man would come in with the monks to hear him speak. When they left, he would leave also. One day, however, he remained behind.

Pai-chang asked him, "Who are you, standing here before me?"

The old man answered, "Indeed, I am not a human being. In the ancient days of Kāshyapa Buddha, I was head priest at this mountain. One day a monk asked me, 'Does the completely enlightened person fall under the law of cause and effect or not?' I replied, 'Such a person does not fall under the law of cause and effect.' With this I was reborn five hundred times as a fox. I beg you to give me a turning word to release me from my life as a fox. Tell me, does the completely enlightened person fall under the law of cause and effect?" Pai-chang said, "The law of cause and effect cannot be evaded." With this, the old man was enlightened.[1]

It cannot be evaded, yet the Law of Karma, and more broadly the Dharma itself remain elusive. Religion, philosophy, and science everywhere pursue the Dharma and seek to understand it. Modern physicists find themselves close to the Buddhist understanding of the law; they see that phenomena are empty, yet not empty, just as the *Cheng-tao ko* says.[2] The further physicists pursue the Dharma, the closer they come to the unknowable. Translate "essential nature" as "energy" and the "possibilities" of essential nature as "tendencies," and you will be talking good physics.[3] (The reverse is not true, however. Emptiness in physics is a phenomenon. The Zen Buddhist will quote the proverb: "Even the sky must be beaten." Emptiness itself must be wiped away.)

So what is meant by Dharma assets? In light of all the meanings of "Dharma," we can understand "Dharma assets" to indicate energy and its tendencies, energy and its inclinations. The bounty of the phenomenal world is matched by the bounteous spirit of the individual. The First Precept and all the precepts are summed up here in Number Eight: "Not Sparing the Dharma Assets." It is the positive reflex of Not Killing. "Don't kill" and "Do encourage life"—these are the same thing.

The assets of the Dharma include money, the test of the pure spirit. There is such a thing as dirty money, and in Kamakura you can launder yours at the sacred spring of the Shinto shrine, Zeniarai Benten. I like this custom, and feel that with honest intention, the money is really purified. Better, however, to keep it the medium of exchange for bread and labor to begin with. Right Livelihood is more than avoiding the business of selling wine to winos. Making money with money is not earning a living, in my view.

The important thing is attitude, to be pure in giving or receiving something, as pure as the act of standing up. When Seisetsu Shūryo Kokushi was roshi of Engaku Monastery in Kamakura, the dojo needed to be rebuilt to accommodate the large number of monks who had gathered to practice. A wealthy merchant brought five hundred pieces of gold, an immense amount of money, for this purpose.

The story varies at this point, but according to the version I heard from Nakagawa Sōen Roshi, Seisetsu Zenji just said, "Okay, I'll take it."

The merchant was miffed that he had not been thanked, so he said, "In that sack are five hundred pieces of gold."

Seisetsu was playing a game of *go* at the time and he looked up again from his board and said simply, "You said that before."

Money energy, work energy, smile energy, jive energy—it is our good fortune, our good karma, to be in a place where we can invest our energy from Dharma to Dharma. Like a tomato plant adding itself to the soil for the sake of other tomato plants, we are agents of vitality spending ourselves freely as that vitality, for that vitality.

So with no more self-consciousness than the tomato

plant, we paint the house, dig in the garden, pound on the typewriter. The wealthy merchant sought recompense by way of thanks for his gift and thus was actually sparing the Dharma assets. Seisetsu Zenji was generous with his teaching, fitting it to the occasion. We can be sure that under other circumstances he would have been unsparing with smiles and words of gratitude. Meister Eckhart said,

> To give a thousand marks of gold to build a church or a cloister would be a great thing, but to give a thousand marks for nothing at all would be a far greater gift.[4]

That is the true spirit of not sparing the Dharma assets.

When Hui-hai was asked about entering the Tao, he said we enter by the danaparamita, the perfection of relinquishment, the perfection of giving over.[5] It is like bowing all the way to the floor.

Yamada Roshi says that bowing is the act of throwing everything away. It is also said that lifting one's hands while prostrate in a bow is the act of lifting the Buddha's feet over one's head. The beginning student may have a hard time accepting all this, as it can seem degrading to human dignity. It is important to understand how the prostration before the altar is equivalent to danaparamita in daily life. There are many stories in Buddhist literature, beginning with the *Jataka Tales*, which teach us the Precept of Not Sparing the Dharma Assets as complete relinquishment:

> Jimon was a nun who lived in Japan in the 18th century. One cold night, a thief came to her hut looking for something. Without getting excited at all, she arose and said, "How miserable it must have been to cross the fields and mountains to come here on such a cold night—wait a minute and I'll get you something warm." She made some gruel for him and had him sit down by the fire. She said to him, "I

have given up the world so I don't have anything of value, but please take anything you want. In exchange, I have something to tell you. I've been looking at you, and it seems to me that whatever work you do, you will not have a hard time making a living—so isn't it a shame that you have fallen into such a low state and disgraced not only yourself but your family as well? Please reform your outlook and give up this business of burglary. Take whatever I have and sell it to get capital to do any kind of work which suits your ability—you'll be much easier in mind." The thief was so impressed that he left without taking anything.[6]

Jimon was a true student of our founding teacher:

Bodhidharma said, "Self-nature is subtle and mysterious. In the genuine, all-pervading Dharma, not being stingy about a single thing is called the Precept of Not Sparing the Dharma Assets."

In the genuine, all-pervading Dharma, there is a woman here, an algaroba tree there, a lava rock here, a cat there. Each individual comes forth as the Tathagata, coming forth as its own being, with nothing identical to it anywhere at any time. Each individual is teaching and relinquishing everything. The universe is ablaze with wealth, flashing through each of its beings. Understanding this, Jimon could share the Dharma assets.

Like the other precepts, the Eighth Precept is not basically cautionary. It affirms what has been true from the beginning. The wealthy merchant violated this precept, we can say, or acted in ignorance of it, by presuming that money was something separately his own to be shared with Enkakuji. Actually, his act was like sharing a smile, or giving a flower to a child. But don't suppose that a flower will pay for our sesshin costs. All things in proportion.

In the *Fukan Zazengi*, Dogen Zenji says, "The treasury of precious things opens of itself. You may take them and use them any way you like."[7] This is a koan. How do you respond? Does this mean that you can explode a nuclear device or set an oil refinery on fire just because you feel like it? Bodhidharma and Dogen Zenji speak from their essential ground in *this* world.

Here is how the whole matter comes into focus:

> Dogen Zenji said, "One phrase, one verse—that is the ten thousand things and one hundred grasses; one dharma, one realization—that is all Buddhas and Ancestral Teachers. Therefore, from the beginning, there has been no stinginess at all."

"Ten thousand things" is the Chinese way of saying "everything." How is it that one phrase, or one verse, can be everything? As Nakagawa Sōen Roshi used to say about Yun-men's famous one-word phrase, rendered in Japanese as *Kanshiketsu* (dried shit stick), just "*kan*" is enough, just "*kkk*" is enough. Sometimes the old teachers shouted "*Katsu!*," sometimes they held up a flower. Blake asks if you can see the world in a grain of sand.

The same truth is found on the other side of the ledger. "Grasses" is shorthand in Zen literature for delusions and attachments. One phrase, and the one hundred, or the 84,000 delusions and attachments are made manifest.

When the Buddha held forth a flower before his assembly, that was a full and complete presentation of the entire universe and of all the teachings of all the Buddhas and Ancestral Teachers.[8] The primrose by the river's brim, the child splashing in her bath, the cat miaowing at the door, that cloud hanging over Haleakala, all these are unsparing of the teaching.

When our delusions and attachments of *mine* and *yours*, *ours* and *theirs*, get in the way, we are dualistic in our sparing and sharing, and we cannot testify to the presentation of a flower. This kind of division in attitude is the fundamental delusion, as Yasutani Roshi has said. See where it leads us in national affairs, with the poor becoming angrier, and the rich becoming more arrogant. See where it leads us in international affairs, with each country protecting its own while pressing outward against all the others, as the world shrinks with its burgeoning technology. In our own communities and families sometimes we may tend to protect ourselves in subgroups without much generosity for other subgroups. It is easy to criticize the world, hard to see how we have contributed to its suffering by our own violation of this precept.

Our First Vow "Though the many beings are numberless, I vow to save them" is a paraphrase of the Eighth Precept, but with attachments to concepts of mine and yours, it is meaningless, for you do not really perceive the sights and sounds of the world:

> Ti-tsang asked Hsiu-shan, "Where have you come from?"
>
> Hsiu-shan said, "From the South."
>
> Ti-tsang said, "How is Buddhism in the South these days?"
>
> Hsiu-shan said, "It is widely discussed."
>
> Ti-tsang said, "Planting my rice field and growing rice is better than that."
>
> Hsiu-shan said, "How can you save all beings of the Three Worlds in such a way?"
>
> Ti-tsang said, "What do you mean by the 'Three Worlds?'"[9]

Hsiu-shan glibly parrots a phrase from his conceptional understanding of Buddhism. The Three Worlds, in his context, are those of desire, form, and no form, and he is caught up in the abstraction that surely it is our duty to get out into society and discuss Buddhism, to encourage its practice. How can you fulfill your vow to save all beings in all dimensions just grubbing in the mud? Hsiu-shan saw those beings as entities "out there."

Ti-tsang was one of the Buddhist heroes in the T'ang period, the golden age of Zen. He was the teacher of Fa-yen, and renowned for his incisive way of using the words of his students as a judo player uses the strength of an opponent. He dissolved the roots of Hsiu-shan's delusions, to use Abe Masao Sensei's cogent expression.[10] His metaphor was the rice paddy, but his action was an altogether generous presentation of the Dharma.

Lots of people pay lip service to such abstractions as truth, justice, peace, love, saving all beings, and so on. But if they do not speak and act from the empty center that is so potent with generosity, they are used by their abstractions, truth becomes truth for *us*; justice becomes justice for *us*; and all beings become only our group, our class, our nation, or whatever. The fact that all beings are already saved is thus obscured.

True sharing is the act of the tomato plant or the plankton, the mind of the universe where nothing is spared. When you are caught up in abstractions, such as the Three Worlds, you are caught up in self-centeredness. Realizing one dharma as universal Dharma, a wild flower as heaven itself—that is freedom from abstraction. Then you may recite the "Great Vows for All" simply as a confirmation of your own unsparing mind. Return to Mu, and your act of lifting your spoon to your mouth will be a fulfillment of this precept.

CHAPTER TEN

The Ninth
Grave Precept

Not Indulging in Anger

Some years ago, when Tibetan teachers first appeared in Hawaii, one of them cornered me at a reception and asked, "What do Zen teachers say about anger?"

I replied, "Fundamentally, there is no anger, and no one to get angry." He gave me a strange look, but said nothing.

Now I must explore all the things that were left unsaid in that truncated conversation. Reflecting on my reply, I think I was a bit like Hui the Recluse, who said, "Nothing special." When this was reported to Ch'ang-sha, he composed the following poem:

> You who sit on the top of a hundred-foot pole,
> Although you have entered the way, it is not yet
>   genuine.
> Take a step from the top of the pole
> And the universe in the ten directions will be your
>   entire body.[1]

The one on the top of the pole is like the Buddha after his great realization—before he sought out his friends. *It* is all empty, but, as the *Heart Sutra* says, emptiness is also form.[2] If there is no anger, what is this that rises in my heart when someone mocks a Buddhist ceremony? I reflect on my own bitter experiences with anger, a story that begins long ago:

In 1942, the novelist Philip Wylie published a book called *Generation of Vipers*, which was a distillation of his anger about the women who had frustrated his process of maturing. When I read this book after the war, it elevated to my consciousness the emasculation I had suffered in my own boyhood as I attempted to cope with dominating women, my mother to some degree, but more particularly one of my grandmothers.

However, though I was aware of my feelings, I could not work with them, and I recall at age thirty-three sitting in my first sesshin in a Japanese monastery, devoting my full attention to cursing my mother over a misunderstanding about money, in which I thought she believed that I had not behaved honorably. The incident was a full two years past at that time.

I understood very little Japanese, and so could not ask for help with my problem at those sesshins, but a little later, on the same pilgrimage, I sat with another teacher who gave me the koan Mu. Settling into Mu helped me to find a floor that was deeper than my emotions. This was my earliest experience of the therapeutic effect of proper zazen. On returning to the United States, I was able to reach a better relationship with my mother, for my memory no longer took over my brain, and I could respond to her directly.

Sitting there on my cushions at Enkakuji in 1950, murmuring "My damned mother" as a pernicious anti-mantra, was an exercise in self-identity that was the best I could do at the time. I knew very well that I was not seeing beyond a self-centered place, and I tried to return to my koan whenever I caught myself indulging in my fixation, but the emotion was as powerful as a forest fire, and I could not cope with it at all.

My problem was simply that I was immature. The Three Poisons are identified as such because they are indeed poisonous, the most deadly forms of childishness. When we were children and adolescents, we hated in self-defense, and maintained ourselves and our groups with violent words and even violent actions. We were in the process of creating our identities. Now we are adult, but perhaps we still feel that adolescent protectiveness, and when someone appears with harsh words of criticism, it is only with difficulty, if at all, that we can acknowledge the appearance of the avatar of the Buddha. The *Ts'ai-ken t'an* says:

> If treacherous talk is constantly in your ears, and unwanted thoughts are constantly in your mind, you can turn these about and use them as whetstones to enhance your practice. If every word that came to your ears were agreeable, and all things in your mind were pleasant, then your whole life would be poisoned and wasted.[3]

We are not seeking merely to quiet our minds, but to practice. This means *using* what comes up in outward circumstances or in our heads. Whatever happens can serve as a reminder. A friend of mine quotes the Zen teacher Seung Sahn: "The one who praises you is a thief. The one who criticizes you is your true friend." Everything is a whetstone.

Neglect of whetstone practice in international politics leads to world conflict. "He can't do that to me" becomes "They can't do that to us." Speaking of anger, it makes me angry to watch world leaders behave like willful children. And yet they are speaking for their people, for us all.

Women ground down from childhood by patriarchal domination can perhaps empathize with the suffering and anger I experienced in early days, though our situations were different in quality and degree. I feel that my personal history makes it easier for me to understand the imperatives of feminism than it might be for a man who grew up in a family where women conformed to conventional stereotypes. But, male or female, we all have to acknowledge and work with our anger.

Here is how a poet worked with his:

> When [Robert Louis Stevenson] saw a dog being mistreated, he at once interposed, and when the owner resented his interference and told him, "It's not your dog," he cried out, "It's *God's* dog and I'm here to protect it." [4]

Stevenson's famous letter responding to slander of Father Damien is another example of righteous anger. Damien was a famous priest who served lepers on the Island of Molokai. A Protestant minister in Honolulu had written a private letter about him, which was then published. It accused Damien of excessive pride, an ungovernable temper, and even sexual misconduct. Stevenson responded with an open letter accusing the minister in turn of sectarian jealousy. [5]

Where does righteousness stop and self-righteousness begin? Incisive, emphatic correction of someone else is not necessarily indulgence in self-protection, though of course there may be elements of one in the other. Stevenson is said to have regretted his intemperate language after his letter was published.

Yasutani Roshi's hot temper comes to mind here: he boiled over with rage at the conventional, modern Soto denial of the importance of realization. On many occasions, even among his own students who agreed with him, he would raise the subject with fierce face and hot words.

> I hear there are fellows who are called professors in Buddhist universities who indiscriminately pour coarse tea into Dogen's Dharma, cheating and bewildering beginners and long-practicing Zen people as well. They are an unforgiv-

able gang of devils, great thieves of heaven and earth, and should be termed vermin in the body of the lion. They do not realize that they are pitiable people, slandering the Three Treasures, and they must fall into hell after their death. That is because they do not go to true masters for guidance, and are ruined by mistaken scholastic interpretations of Zen. We cannot regret this too much.[6]

I can picture the old roshi writing this out, his brush slashing over the paper, his mouth stern and his eyes glinting. He was like Fudō Myō-ō, the unmovable king of subtle wisdom in the Buddhist pantheon, sitting in the midst of flames, red in the face, eyes bulging, and with the fiercest expression imaginable.

In the iconography of Buddhism, Fudo is the reflex of Kanzeon, the incarnation of mercy and compassion. Fudo and Kanzeon have the same function, as did Yasutani Roshi, to save all beings.

Here is a test—how do you reconcile the anger of Fudo and Yasutani Roshi with words of the *Hsin-hsin ming*?

> To set up what you like against what you dislike:
> This is the disease of the mind.
> When the deep meaning (of the Way) is not understood,
> Peace of mind is disturbed to no purpose.[7]

Surely Yasutani Roshi condemning the scholar-priests of Komazawa University was setting up what he liked against what he disliked. Was his mind diseased? Not a bit—no more than yours if you see a violation of common decency, and respond with hot words and a fierce expression. Yasutani Roshi understood the deep meaning of the Way, and his peace of mind was unmoved—perhaps that would be the difference between his anger and yours. But in both cases you and he are saying, in effect, "This is true; that is not true." The passion is the purity of the Tathagata coming forth, and the motive is the mercy of Kanzeon.

> Bodhidharma said, "Self-nature is subtle and mysterious. In the realm of the selfless Dharma, not contriving reality for the self is called the Precept of Not Indulging in Anger."

When there is a bit of self to defend, that is a violation of this precept. Yasutani Rōshi was protecting the Dharma, and he didn't care about himself at all. His temple was tiny, his robe was shabby and worn, and his time and energy were devoted to conveying the mind. The *Hsin-hsin ming* is talking about self-centered preferences and prejudices, judgments that relate to the *me* that exploits people and things.

Two years ago, when we were negotiating with Maui County about a variance, I asked for volunteers to appear in my place, saying that I had a reputation in town for being pushy, and I didn't want to jeopardize the proceedings by showing my face. Someone asked, "Doesn't it make you angry to hear that people think you are pushy?" I was surprised. Twenty years ago I might have gotten angry at such a thing, I suppose. I must be getting old.

In the exigencies of the moment, you may not know that you are responding in a self-centered way. It is important to cultivate as best you can your own empty ground of action and expression, so that you are not blown about by the reactions of others. Then when you come forth with your response, you will learn clearly whether or not you are being self-indulgent, and this can be your whetstone.

In our koan study, we find that Chien-yuan responded angrily to his teacher's uncompromising presentation, and deepened his practice thereafter to the place where he could finally echo his teacher's wisdom.

Tao-wu and Chien-yuan went to a house to pay condolences. Chien-yuan rapped on the coffin and asked, "Living or dead?"

Tao-wu said, "I won't say living; I won't say dead."

Chien-yuan said, "Why won't you say?"

Tao-wu said, "I won't say."

On their way back, Chien-yuan said, "Your Reverence, please tell me right away. If you don't, I will hit you."

Tao-wu said, "I'll allow you to hit me, if you like, but I won't say." Chien-yuan hit him.

Later, after Tao-wu passed away, Chien-yuan went to Shih-shuang and told him this story. Shih-shuang said, "I won't say living; I won't say dead."

Chien-yuan said, "Why won't you say?"

Shih-shuang said, "I won't say! I won't say!" With these words, Chien-yuan was enlightened.[8]

The old teachers were passionate about the Dharma. Do you think Nan-ch'uan was angry when he killed the cat? I am sure that he showed an angry face.[9]

Don't misunderstand. The Dharma of no-self is quiet when nothing comes up, and active when things appear, but Nan-ch'uan's action was not just a spontaneous response. Mere spontaneity is not the Way. Peace lies at the root of the enlightened response, and guidance is its quality.

> Dogen Zenji said, "Not advancing, not retreating, not real, not empty. There is an ocean of bright clouds. There is an ocean of solemn clouds."

This passage is full of points for koan study, and I am reluctant to touch it. The reference is to the Middle Way, the Tathagata coming forth in this world. What is "not advancing, not retreating?" The Tathagata originates in that unmoving place. What is "not real, not empty"? The *Cheng-tao ko* clarifies this in speaking of the Mani-jewel:

> It operates our sight, hearing, smell, taste, sensation, awareness;
> And all of these are empty, yet not empty.[10]

What are the "ocean of bright clouds" and the "ocean of solemn clouds"? I notice here on Maui that when the sky is overcast, the Chinese thrush sings, and when it is sunny, the cardinal and mynah birds sing. Sometimes solemn, sometimes bright, the thrush teaches, the mynah teaches. When it rains, I run for cover. When it is fine, I take my dog for a walk. If someone complains, I try to adjudicate. Sometimes, however, I must raise my voice and say, "Cut that out!" When there is no advance or retreat in my heart of hearts, then I am truly teaching. As the *Diamond Sutra* says, in effect, you come forth as the Tathagata when you come from your original dwelling place, emptiness itself.[11]

In sum, this precept too is not a mere moral injunction. Anger and love are names for certain tendencies of energy. If you cannot feel anger at all, then you are blocking your own creativity. That needs correction. Thich Nhat Hanh says:

> Treat your anger with the utmost respect and tenderness, for it is no other than yourself. Do not suppress it—simply be aware of it. Awareness is like the sun. When it shines on things, they are transformed. When you are aware that you are angry, your anger is transformed. If you destroy anger, you destroy the Buddha, for Buddha and Mara are of the same essence. Mindfully dealing with anger is like taking the hand of a little brother.[12]

That is an expression of bright clouds. What about solemn clouds? William Blake says (translate his term "Intellect" as *prajñā*):

Men are admitted into Heaven not because they have curbed & governd their Passions or have No Passions but because they have Cultivated their Understandings. The Treasures of Heaven are not Negations of Passion but Realities of Intellect from which all the Passions Emanate Uncurbed in their Eternal Glory.[13]

I'll let old Chao-chou have the last say:

Chao-chou: Buddhahood is passion and passion is Buddhahood.
    Monk: In whom does Buddha cause passion?
    Chao-chou: Buddha causes passion in all of us.
    Monk: How do we get rid of it?
    Chao-chou: Why should we get rid of it?[14]

CHAPTER ELEVEN

The Tenth
Grave Precept

*Not Defaming
the Three Treasures*

The Three Treasures are fundamental to Buddhist practice, and, apart from their sectarian tone, fundamental to all religious practice. They are, of course, the Buddha, the Dharma, and the Sangha: enlightenment, the truth, and harmony. Not defaming them is the path of understanding them fully, keeping them clear in our minds, and presenting them in our lives.

The Buddha is the Enlightened One, the historical Buddha to begin with, but also the nature of the universe and of all universes, the wisdom of earthworms and the dirt in which they have their being. The Dharma is doctrine, and also the reality it describes, vast and fathomless, clearly in focus with the sudden cry of a gecko in an early Hawaiian evening. The sangha is harmony—of the Buddha's disciples to begin with, but also of all beings in a magnificent network of interrelationships—the balance of stars and the symbiosis of termites and their parasites. Sangha is also the harmony of doctrine and enlightenment, phenomena and the absolute, form and emptiness —the *Heart Sutra* expounded in the rainbow playing about Manoa Falls.[1]

Understanding the Three Treasures fully is a matter of experiencing them. It may be clear that "Buddha-nature

pervades the whole universe"[2]; it is everywhere; it cannot
be defamed—but what kind of clarity is that? Perhaps it is a
bit abstract and intellectual. It may not be so clear that
Buddha-nature is moral.

Take, for example, Yun-men's famous saying, "Every
day is a good day."[3] Once during a question period a student
asked me, "Could Yun-men rightfully have said, 'Every
day is a bad day?'" I said, "No," and went on to point out
that Hakuin Zenji said, "All beings by nature are Buddha,"
not "All beings by nature are Mara."[4]

When you forget yourself completely, just once, you are
incredibly enlarged, and the way of compassion is opened.
Mara is then clearly an error, Good is the Tao, and you find
your home in the Three Treasures.

The Three Pure Precepts then set forth your path in the
world:

> Renounce all evil;
> Practice all good;
> Save the many beings.[5]

Enlightenment, the Tao, and harmony become personal
motives. You are disciplined, and altogether outgoing.
The Ten Grave Precepts are guidelines to show you how to
proceed.

The Ten Grave Precepts, the Three Pure Precepts, and
the Three Vows of Refuge in the Three Treasures are for-
mally integrated into the practice in the ceremony of Jukai,
in which the student vows before the assembly and the
roshi (standing in for Shakyamuni), to make these Sixteen
Bodhisattva Precepts "my own," and to acknowledge, "I
am a disciple of Shakyamuni Buddha." The roshi then
hands the student a *ketchimyaku*, literally "blood pulse" cer-
tificate, showing his or her lineage back to Shakyamuni
Buddha, and a *rakusu*, an abbreviated apron-like garment,
representing the robe of the Buddha, which the student
then wears at all Zen Buddhist meetings. It is a solemn rit-

ual, and serves to link right thinking and right action to the devotional spirit and to religious practice.

At most Western centers, students who elect the Jukai Ceremony are encouraged to sew their own rakusus. This is in keeping with the ancient Buddhist tradition of making one's own robe. The new monk would take off all clothing, and walk naked to the town dump and there pick out scraps of cloth, bleach them, sew them together to form a robe, and then dye the robe with the most inexpensive dyes. Sewing one's own rakusu, also with scraps of cloth, echoes and helps us to personify the wholehearted religious integrity of our ancestors, taking off the old clothing of the Three Poisons, putting on the new clothing of the Buddha.

Hakuin Zenji wrote: "This very body is the Buddha."[6] Wearing the Buddha's clothing and eating from the Buddha's bowls (as we acknowledge in our mealtime sutras[7]) we affirm the Buddha's wisdom and the precepts that naturally arise from it, as we nurse our children or drive to the office.

The Three Treasures are affirmed at the beginning of Zen Buddhist sutra services, when we recite the *Ti Sarana*, the "Refuge Gatha," which is the heart of all Buddhist ceremony—Mahayana, Vajrayana, and Theravada. Senzaki Nyogen Sensei always recited this gatha in the original Pali, by way of expressing the unity of all Buddhism:

> Buddham saranam gacchāmi;
> Dahmmam saranam gacchāmi;
> Sangham saranam gacchāmi.

Usually the gatha is translated:

> I take refuge in the Buddha;
> I take refuge in the Dharma;
> I take refuge in the Sangha.

The intention of the original is affirmation of Buddha, Dharma, and Sangha as my home. Each time we mindfully recite this gatha, we are vowing to receive, maintain, and manifest the Three Treasures as ourselves. It is the Jukai ritual in brief, renewed at each of our ceremonies, together with all Buddhists everywhere.

Taking refuge in the Three Treasures is like Jui-yen calling to his master:

> Every day Jui-yen called to himself, "Master!"
> And he replied, "Yes."
> "Be alert!"
> "Yes, I will."
> "Don't be deceived by others!"
> "No, I won't." [8]

This case is sometimes misunderstood as simple self-correction, as someone at the end of the day might reflect on mistakes and resolve to do better. Such meditation is fine, but it is not Jui-yen's practice. He is receiving, maintaining, and presenting the Three Treasures. He is saying in three ways, "I come back home."

Jui-yen was, however, explicitly not repeating "Buddha, Dharma, and Sangha," and was warning himself not to be dependent on anything or anybody. Thus his words are vows that go deeper than any formal promise in the temple. The "don't-know mind" that underlies and infuses the Three Treasures keeps Jui-yen inspired and straight. In fact, there is a risk of defaming the Three Treasures by taking refuge in them. As Wu-men said, "If you just utter the name Buddha, you should rinse out your mouth for three days. If you are such a fellow, and you hear someone say, 'This very mind is Buddha' you will cover your ears and run from the room." [9]

This is not a license for secular rejection of ceremony, but weight to balance the *Mādhyamika*. "The Buddha is not the Buddha, therefore he is called Buddha," Professor D. T. Suzuki used to say, paraphrasing the *Diamond Sutra*.

> Chao-chou addressed his assembly and said, "I do not like
> to hear the word 'Buddha.'"
> A monk asked, "Then how does Your Reverence teach
> others?"
> Chao-chou said, "Buddha. Buddha." [10]

"When you meet the Buddha, you kill the Buddha"—
kill that controlling thought. [11] But Buddha is also our precious teacher, without whom and *which* our practice would
be barren. All archetypes and metaphors are like this. If I
cannot say "sweet," I cannot speak of ohia honey. If I cannot
say "red," I cannot describe Kilauea erupting at night. But
"sweet" and "red" can turn into entities and control us.
"Sweet" triggers "sentimental," "red" triggers "communist," and thus we are used by words.

The other day, at a meeting of Buddhists from several
different denominations held at Koko An, someone asked,
with reference to Bodhidharma on our altar, "Do you say
'Saint Dharma'?" I said, "No," and because the questioner
spoke Japanese, I gave the Japanese title, "Daruma Dai-
shi"—"Great Teacher (Bodhi)Dharma." The question remains: Is there a difference between "Saint" and "Great
Teacher?" Saint Mary is in heaven and listens compassion-
ately to our prayers, answering them in our hearts. Where is
Bodhidharma? I would not say "Heaven," I think. And I
would say that he speaks from, rather than to or in, our
hearts. But really, the difference lies in cultural and religious attitudes. It is also possible to say that Mary is our
true nature, and Daruma responds to our innermost needs.

> Bodhidharma said, "Self-nature is subtle and mysterious.
> In the realm of the One, not holding dualistic concepts of
> ordinary beings and sages is called the Precept of Not De-
> faming the Three Treasures."

If you truly abide in the Three Treasures, if they are intimately a part of your delight in reciting sutras, eating ce-

real, and chatting with your friends, then there is nothing to be called ordinary, nothing to be called sagacious. When you are hungry, you eat; when you are tired, you take a nap.

What is the difference between such a way and the path of one who is unconsciously projecting past karma, beating his kids and getting drunk, who also eats when he is hungry and rests when tired? It is the difference between having a practice and not having one. It is the difference between accepting the Bohisattva Precepts as one's own, and not accepting them.

Practicing fulfillment of the Three Refuges, you find there is nothing outside Buddha-nature. The one who beats his kids and gets drunk has no confidence in his Buddha-nature, we can say. The violation of the precept comes when you deny your unity with Buddha-nature, and put yourself high or low by some standard. People who suffer social prejudice, such as the Harijan in India, the Burakumin in Japan, or Blacks in the United States and South Africa or convicts in any culture, can take Buddhahood personally without any feeling of inferiority. A philanthropist can take refuge in the Three Treasures without a thought of generosity.

This is practice. We know Bodhidharma only as an enlightened old man, but he too practiced hard all his life, we can be sure. He could not express wisdom in his youth the way he did after he arrived in China. We share Bodhidharma's youthful tribulations in our own immature years, and take inspiration from his great mature teaching.

Be careful. Old man Bodhidharma must not be allowed to get the upper hand. There is no ordinary being or sage, no leader and follower, no roshi and student. Not Defaming the Three Treasures is a matter of finding them in your heart mind. The roshi must be ready to hear that he is a male chauvinist. The student must be ready to hear equally disagreeable stuff. Thus we practice open expression in the Diamond Sangha with communications workshops, sharing meetings, women's and men's rap groups, and business decisions by consensus.

I am working at the bench, polishing the Three Jewels. You are working at the same bench, polishing the same Three Jewels. This is the most important work in the world.

> Dogen Zenji said, "The teisho of the actual body is the harbor and the weir. This is the most important thing in the world. Its virtue finds its home in the ocean of essential nature. It is beyond explanation. We just accept it with respect and gratitude."

Here Dogen Zenji is seen at his most difficult. By "teisho of the actual body," he is pointing to the way of the Bodhisattva, something not to be taken casually, and not to be fixed in printed words. The Buddha's own life, the marvel of how things are—rivers, trees, animals, people—and the identity of the Tathagata with your act of standing up and putting on clothes, all are brought into focus as the sermon of the actual body: the harbor and the weir, where the boats gather, where the fish gather. There is nothing more important.

"Its virtue finds its home in the ocean of essential nature." This is the act of taking refuge as, for example, we lie down to go to sleep. The "Pure Conduct" chapter of the *Hua-yen Sutra* offers this gatha for the end of the day:

> When it is time to stop and sleep,
> I vow with all beings
> to find peaceful retirement
> and a heart that is undisturbed. [12]

The ocean of essential nature is the nature of Buddha extending through the whole universe, with each and every thing totally void. I vow to embody that tranquility. How? Well, for one thing, try reciting that gatha at bedtime. That is a good place to start.

"It is beyond explanation." The Dharma is incomparably profound and minutely subtle. When we say that it is a presentation of all the possibilities of essential nature in full flower as they are, intimately interacting, with each being perfectly reflecting and interpenetrating each other being, we are just explaining. The Dharma is not philosophy.

"We just accept it with respect and gratitude." The sangha is the harmony and indeed the identity of all beings and their karma with the absolute and unmoving Buddha. I bow in gratitude. There is nothing more to say.

CHAPTER TWELVE
Eating the Blame

At the monastery of Fūgai Ekun, ceremonies delayed preparation of the noon meal one day, and when they were over, the cook took up his sickle and hurriedly gathered vegetables from the garden. In his haste, he lopped off part of a snake, and, unaware that he had done so, threw it into the soup pot with the vegetables.

At the meal, the monks thought they had never tasted such delicious soup, but the Roshi himself found something remarkable in his bowl. Summoning the cook, he held up the head of the snake, and demanded, "What is this?"

The cook took the morsel, saying, "Oh, thank you, Roshi," and immediately ate it.[1]

This is one of the many mondo in Zen literature that teaches us how to use a challenge, and not be used by it in the ordinary way. What would an ordinary reply have been? "Oh, the ceremonies went on so long I had to hurry up to prepare dinner. I didn't notice that I had part of a snake in the soup. Please excuse me."

A very poor response, you will agree. But the cook in our story had nothing to defend. He did not for one moment

105

take the roshi's challenge as an accusation. He took the matter from there and gave everyone a wonderful teisho.

How do you handle challenge? You have two options. One is to defend and the other is to dance. There are many kinds of defense: to accuse the other, to excuse oneself, or simply to stand mute. In any case, the defense is not a dance. There is no teisho: that is, there is no presentation, no teaching.

The dance, too, is of many kinds. Sometimes there is an opportunity, as in this case, to make the whole matter disappear. Sometimes you can bundle it up neatly and toss it back. Sometimes a laugh is enough. Certainly we may be sure that this mondo ended with a laugh. Sometimes the dance can be a question, "What is your opinion?" or "How would you handle it?"

Ching-ch'ing asked a monk, "What is that sound outside?"

The monk said, "The sound of rain dripping."

Ching-ch'ing said, "Ordinary people are upside down, falling into delusion about themselves, and pursuing outside objects."

The monk said, "How would you handle it, Your Reverence?"

Ching-ch'ing said, "I am on the brink of falling into delusion about myself."

The monk said, "What do you mean, 'On the brink of falling into delusion about yourself'?"

Ching-ch'ing said, "To attain to the world of emptiness may not be so difficult, but to express the bare substance is hard."[2]

The monk had not the foggiest notion of what Ching-ch'ing was talking about but he danced very nicely, leading Ching-ch'ing on. Another person might have been intimidated and reacted protectively with Ching-ch'ing's first admonition, and we would have been deprived of the full teisho. The monk came back a second time too, you will notice. Yasutani Roshi used to say, "You should always ask"—meaning, "Speak up when things are not clear and get them clarified."

The readiness to dance is freedom from karma. Once when I was in doubt about what to tell people about my religion, I asked R. H. Blyth what he would say if someone asked him if he were a Buddhist. He said, "I would say, 'I am if you're not.'" Very witty, but also very defensive, I think. The other person is defeated and that is not the purpose of the dance.

Freedom from karma does not mean that I transcend cause and effect. It means I acknowledge that my perceptions are empty and I am no longer anxious to keep my ego bastion in good repair. Does a stranger walk through the ruined walls? Welcome stranger! How about a dance?

The readiness to dance is the readiness to learn, the openness to growth.

Tan-hsia asked a monk, "Where have you come from?"

The monk said, "From the foot of the mountain."

Tan-hsia asked, "Have you eaten your rice?"

The monk said, "Yes, I have."

Tan-hsia asked, "What sort of fellow would give you rice to eat? Did he have open eyes?" The monk said nothing.

Later, Ch'ang-ching said to Pao-fu, "Surely it is one's role to repay Buddhas and Ancestral Teachers by giving people food. How is it that the one who served rice had no eyes?"

Pao-fu said, "Server and receiver are both blind."

Ch'ang-ching said, "Is the one who makes the utmost charitable effort nonetheless blind?"

Pao-fu said, "Do you call me blind?"[3]

"Do you call me blind?" What a terrible response! Yet this is the kind of response we are forever giving in the face of challenge. What is it that gets in the way of the dance?

Me! Me! Me! You mustn't call me blind. That's an insult. I won't stand for it.

What won't stand for it? All those skandhas are empty, you know. All those perceptions are vacant. Empty, yet not empty. What is the form of that emptiness? Well, that would be a dance in response to Ch'ang-ching's final question, "Is the one who makes the utmost charitable effort nonetheless blind?" What would you reply? Yuan-wu, editor of *The Blue Cliff Record*, offered his own response: "Blind!" said Yuan-wu.[4] That's a good one.

The dancer is the one who forgets herself in the dance. "Do you call me blind?" is a very self-conscious response. Pao-fu went on to become a great teacher, but at this point, he was still green. He was frozen in himself.

When I was in the Upward Bound program at the University of Hawaii, I tried to get the high school students to act out parts in the novel they were reading. Despite their assignment to prepare their parts, they stood at the front of the room, books in hand, and read aloud with no intonation at all, " 'Where are you going,' he asked."

They had not learned to be free of themselves. They had not learned to unite with the matter at hand. Look at Marcel Marceau, the great French mime. There is no Marceau to be seen, only a kite flyer, only a butterfly catcher, only a prisoner with walls closing in. He dances with the circumstances, forgetting himself.

Notice that when Marceau forgets himself, he becomes altogether unique. There is no one like him in the whole universe. But if you defend yourself, you are dull, no different from anyone else.

One of my colleagues remarked to me, "When I meet a student in dokusan, I am meeting my own master." What happens in dokusan? We both of us forget ourselves, I would hope. If you don't know, you say, "I don't know." If I don't know, I will say so. Sometimes students point out aspects of koans I did not notice before. Sometimes people point out ways I could be more effective as a teacher, and this is very helpful. What do I have to protect?

> Yün-yen was sweeping the grounds. Tao-wu said, "You are working hard, aren't you!"
>
> Yün-yen said, "You should know that there is someone who does not work hard."
>
> Tao-wu said, "Is that so? You mean there is a second moon?"
>
> Yün-yen held up his broom and asked, "What number of moons is this?" Tao-wu said nothing.[5]

Merrily these two Dharma brothers, who were also biological brothers, tossed the wicker ball of wisdom lightly back and forth. They were bringing out the Dharma, each in turn. When the mondo was over, Tao-wu said nothing further. But how they must have grinned at each other.

Contrast this kind of confrontation with the usual sort. The drama plays on and on, "He said this, and I said that. I should have said this other thing, and then he might have said—and then I would say. . . ." Bah! There is no end to it.

This is the problem with defensiveness. It has no end. Ultimately, however, in the oxygen tent, there is no defense. We know this deeply and are frightened of it. So we hold off the acknowledgment as long as possible. But really, there is nothing to defend. There is nothing to protect. There is nothing to depend upon.

> Kuei-shan asked Yang-shan, "Suppose someone asks you, 'How about one who says that all beings are in a disorderly karmic consciousness and have no base to rely upon?' How would you treat such a person?"
>
> Yang-shan said, "If such a person appeared, I would call to him. When he turns his head, instantly I would say, 'What is that?' I would wait while he hesitates, and then I

would say, 'There is not only disorderly karmic consciousness, but no base to rely upon.'"
    Kuei-shan said, "Oh, good."[6]

This is the great joke of Zen. It is the great joke of the
universe. There is no absolute at all, and that is the absolute. Enlightenment is practice, as Dogen Zenji said.[7] And
what is practice? Getting on with it. When you defend, you
are blocking the practice. When you dance, you are getting
on with it.

Lightness and heaviness form the contrast we find between those who can dance and those who are preoccupied
with themselves. Lightness comes with the experience that
one's center is the great void itself. This is the place of great
peace. Like the Buddha emerging from beneath the Bodhi
tree, you come forth from the experience of pure emptiness
into the sangha, into the dance of samsara.

Sangha is a treasure of the Buddha Tao, ranking with enlightenment and the truth. Singing and dancing are the
voice of the Dharma; cooking and gardening are the voice of
the Buddha. Sangha is the complementarity of unity and
diversity, of emptiness and form. Sangha is the story of the
Buddha, lived out in our work together.

The sangha ideal is our guide through the complexities
of people in combination. Everybody is different, and so
misunderstandings arise. With our realization of pure emptiness, with our sense that nothing really matters, we find
true devotion because we no longer worry about ourselves.
The great potential of the *Dharmakāya* becomes our own
unimpeded great action. Differences become configura-
tions we can use and our collective energy can be focused on
the task.

    Let's get on with it.

CHAPTER THIRTEEN

A Note on Samu

Although the Sino-Japanese word *samu* is used at most Western Zen centers, it is mentioned only once, to my knowledge, in English Zen literature—in Satō and Nishimura's *Unsui*, where it is amusingly pictured with a rather inadequate caption.[1] Theory has not yet caught up to practice in Western Buddhism! To examine the term and its traditional usage may clarify the function of samu for Western Zen students.

The etymology of "samu" (Chinese: *tso-wu*) is very interesting. It is made up of two characters, *sa* meaning "a work, production, tillage, or harvest," and *mu* "to devote attention to" as primary meaning, and "service, duty, or occupation" as the derived meaning. This second character also means "Buddhist service," in the sense of "sutra service" (the occupation of monks and nuns, so to speak).

When we recall the etymology of *kinhin*, "sutra-walk," it becomes apparent that samu may be understood as "work-service" or "work-sutras." It is the activity or function of religious devotion in work.

This interpretation is in keeping with the importance placed upon samu in Chinese and Japanese monastic tradition. The standard directory of koans, *Kosoku Zenshū Zen-mon Kōan Taikan*, devotes an entire section to samu, and lists over two hundred pertinent cases.[2] Though Professor D. T. Suzuki does not discuss the Sino-Japanese term itself (he translates it as "labor" or "work"), he devotes a full chapter to the subject in *The Training of the Zen Buddhist Monk*,[3] and several pages in his essay "The Meditation Hall" in *Essays in Zen Buddhism* (First Series).[4]

Apparently samu as a term and practice originates in China. Professor Hajime Nakamura does not give a Sanskrit derivation in his *Bukkyōgo Daijiten*,[5] and Suzuki indicates that work as part of monastic training is a distinguishing feature of Chinese Zen.[6] The earliest reference I can find for samu is in the *Platform Sutra*. After Hui-neng had his first interview with Hung-jen, and before he was assigned to the threshing room, he was "sent to do samu with the assembly."[7]

Thus we may assume that the term and the practice were in use a century before Pai-chang, whose saying, "A day of no samu is a day of no eating," is a basic Zen teaching.[8] In fact, in the days of Hung-jen, Chinese Buddhism was not clearly differentiated into sects, and samu may actually not have had a distinctively Zen origin. I cannot be sure about this.

In any case, Pai-chang, one of the first of our ancestral teachers to confirm the Zen monastery as such, is also revered as a founder of samu. Dogen Zenji writes:

> There was not a single day in the life of Pai-chang, . . . from the time he became attendant of Ma-tsu until the evening of his death, when he did not labor to serve people, and to serve his assembly. To our gratitude, he left the words, "A day of no samu is a day of no eating."
>
> Pai-chang Ch'an-shih was at the extreme of old age, and on occasions of "all-invited" samu, when everybody la-

bored vigorously, the whole assembly felt pain and regret that their teacher should be included in the work party. At last, at one samu time, some monks hid his tools and would not hand them over. That day, Pai-chang did not eat, as compensation for not using mattock and bamboo basket. He said, "A day of no samu is a day of not eating."

Now these words are passed down to us from the Land of Great Peace, and the inner tradition of Rinzai temples and of all Zen temples everywhere is to exercise the function of Pai-chang's profound wisdom.[9]

I understand this profound wisdom to have a number of overlapping implications, both historically and for us today. In earliest Chinese times, samu was the work of supporting the monastery, as well as a sutra service with mattock and sickle. After the T'ang period, begging, large-scale fund raising, and land rentals were generally more important economically than samu, but the religious importance of work was not lost, and as late as Sung times samu was considered one of the four principal components of Zen practice, with zazen, teisho, and dokusan.[10] In thirteenth-century Japan Dogen Zenji wrote extensively about its importance, and it continues to be an integral part of the monastic schedule to this day.

Without samu, Zen Buddhism would be a cult, isolated from daily life. Samu is the extension of sutra services to the garden, the extension of meditation to its function. This is Bodhisattva practice within the temple setting—and for lay students samu is also Bodhisattva work in the world. Suzuki quotes Meister Eckhart, "What a man takes in by contemplation, he pours out in love." Suzuki continues with the observation:

Zen would say, "pours out in work," meaning that work is the concrete actualization of love. Tauler made spin-

ning and shoemaking and other homely duties gifts of the
Holy Ghost. Brother Lawrence made cooking sacramental.
George Herbert wrote:

> Who sweeps a room to thy laws
> Makes that and the action fine.[11]

How does this tradition of work as the actualization of
love bear fruit in our Western sangha? We cannot bear fruit
by cutting off our roots, but at the same time our circumstances are very different from the old monasteries where
monks ate together, bathed together, worked together,
slept together, did zazen together, and even went to the
toilet on signal.[12]

As Western Zen students we find our samu responsibili-
ties have expanded from the traditional functions: to take
care of our homes as well as our temples, to take responsibility for the community as well as for the temple grounds.
But we can learn from a term for samu, *fushin* (Chinese, *p'u-
ch'ing*), which is used when everyone takes part, as on our
sangha workdays. Suzuki writes:

> There was . . . a democratic spirit here in action. The term
> *p'u-ch'ing*, "all invited," means to have every member of the
> Brotherhood on the field, . . . the high as well as the low in
> the hierarchy are engaged in the same kind of work.[13]

The Japanese word "fushin" means "construction" in the
secular language, in the sense of building a house. However, its origin is the Zen term meaning "everyone invited
to turn out for cooperative effort."[14] Construction in the old
days was undoubtedly such communal work.

Chinese and Western cultures are similar in their emphasis upon work, so in taking care of our needs and the needs of
others we draw our inspiration from Pai-chang, rather than

from earlier Indian Buddhist mendicants.[15] In fact, the reformation of Zen Buddhism involved in its move to the West may be seen as a step toward even greater economic independence and social responsibility of the Buddha sangha. Self-reliance and community service are positive virtues in Western tradition, and thus daily samu for residents and our periodic sangha workdays for all members draw from the living roots of both East and West.

At the Koko An Zendo we have been experimenting with community samu. During the 1983 training period, residents worked for three hours each day in agencies devoted to social welfare and social change. Two people worked in a mission on skid row, two in a hospice, two with Native Hawaiians, one in an arboretum, and so on. They brought their experiences back to the center and shared them at meetings scheduled for discussions of how the practice can be applied in daily life.

Samu is zazen engaged in the world's work. We establish the *Bodhimanda*, the Place of the Tao, as we sit in community, and as we work together in community at our temple and in the world. We transmit the Dharma from our founding teachers, not only to ourselves, but to Zen students of the future, and to all beings. This is our sutra dedication to Buddhas throughout space and time. This is the sangha treasure.

The Self

> With the Buddha we have direct affinity;
> with the Buddha we have indirect affinity;
> affinity with the Buddha, Dharma, Sangha,
> realizing eternity, joy, self and purity.
>
> *Enmei Jikku Kannon Gyō*[1]

These lines are from the "Ten Verse Kannon Sutra of Eternal Life." I want to take up the word "self" in the context of this sutra, but first I should say something about the context.

"Eternity" does not refer to beginningless and endless time, but rather to the great timeless void of which we are formed. It is another word for nirvana—not something to be achieved, but the fundamental, potent emptiness that is our essential nature. "Joy" is a word that may also be translated "ease," implying rest and peace.

We have direct affinity with Buddha, Dharma, and sangha, as the tree has affinity with its former seed. We have indirect affinity as the tree does with soil, air, sunlight, and rain. In this karmic relationship we find eternity, joy, purity—and self. What is *self* doing in there?

D. T. Suzuki translates "self" in this sutra as "autonomy."[2] This is correct, but perhaps only one side of the full meaning. With realization, I stand resolute and alone in the universe, but also I stand *one with* the universe. "Autonomy" clarifies standing alone, but not the implication of interpenetration.

When I was younger, I supposed that I had to get rid of my self, and nowadays I sometimes meet people who make the same mistake. Getting rid of the self is not possible, even by suicide I suppose, and the effort is a denial of the Buddha Tao. What we seek, as Yamada Roshi has said, is to forget the self in the act of uniting with something.

The self that is autonomous and also one with all things is the self that is forgotten, not the self that is somehow eliminated. How do you forget the self? In an act—in a task. You don't forget yourself by trying to forget yourself. When you are absorbed in your reading, the words appear in your mind as your own thoughts. When you are absorbed in Mu, then Mu breathes Mu, and the fragrance of incense is sitting there on your cushions. The sound of trees in the wind walks about in kinhin between periods of zazen. The bark of the dog prostrates itself before the altar. Yet these are simply the acts of a Stephen or a Linda.

What then is the role of motive? It is motive that places us in a position to realize that the bulbul sings with my own voice. On the one hand, zazen is full and complete in itself. On the other it is a step-by-step process, a ripening. We forget ourselves in going with this process, as surfers forget themselves in guiding their boards before the wave. The motive and the experience are both absorption in the act, on your cushions or in the world, and whatever analysis and conceptual thinking may have gone before, they are now totally integrated into the purity of action.

The Buddha and all his successors warn us against intellectual structures that confine us to an artificial environment, and against concepts that smear over the living fact of things in themselves. Even the idea of the Buddha must be forgotten: "The Buddha is not the Buddha, therefore he is called Buddha."[3] Therefore she is called Buddha. I am not speaking of the historical fellow here.

The name "Buddha" can be very useful in making a point while teaching, but it can only be given to one who is not controlled by the concept. So we can say: the lover is not a lover, therefore he is called lover; the healer is not a healer, therefore she is called healer.

The task is the act: facing Mu, fixing the roof, drying the cup, or pursuing an idea. When you are lost in the act, the cup dries itself, the hammer swings of itself, the idea is all consuming; and as to Mu, at bedtime he or she stretches out horizontally.

The Christian parallel to the Zen teaching of forgetting the self may be found in the doctrine of obedience. Meister Eckhart begins the first of his "Talks of Instruction":

> True and perfect obedience is a virtue above all virtues. No great work is accomplished without it.[4]

We must understand "obedience" in the way we understand the Buddha. Only when the act is not obedience can we call it obedience.

> Chung Kuo-shih called to his attendant three times, and three times his attendant responded. Kuo-shih said, "I thought I was ungrateful to you, but I find that you are ungrateful to me."[5]

"Grateful" and "ungrateful" are not used in the usual way here, and their usage forms a koan that you will take up in your study. For our purposes, the point is the attendant's clear "echo" of his teacher's call. This is pure obedience, again not in the usual sense. The attendant was completely open and thus in complete harmony with his teacher.

This is precisely the obedience of Ling-yün to the sight of distant peach blossoms. His poem reveals the importance of his experience:

> Some thirty years I sought an expert swordsman.
> How many times leaves fell, how many times branches
>   burst into bud!
> But from the instant I saw the peach flowers blooming,
> From that moment I have had no doubts.[6]

In the last sesshin we held at the old Koko An Zendo, in Kuliouou on Oahu, Nakagawa Sōen Roshi shouted: "*Katsu!*" in the dojo. Like this: [shouting] "*Kaaaatsu!*" I found my own voice joining his, "Aaaaah!" Total obedience.

The word "obedience" carries a lot of associational baggage in our cultures, and in all cultures, I suppose. The creative teacher of religion borrows words and uses them in a fresh way to convey meanings that are not usual. Dogen Zenji is the master of borrowed words. Here is his exposition of the self and its function:

> That the self advances and confirms the myriad things is
>   called delusion
> That the myriad things advance and confirm the self is
>   enlightenment.[7]

"Advances" and "confirms" are not used conventionally here, but the meaning cannot be expressed conventionally. The point is that if Ling-yün had verified the peach blossoms as the most beautiful ones in all China, he would have dominated those flowers and placed them in a conceptual category. This is called delusion. With his spirit of obedience, however, he himself was empty, open to the delicately

subtle dominance of the flowers. They advanced and confirmed him. They were the sparks that lit his Dharma
candle.

"Confirm" is *shō* in Sino-Japanese, literally, "prove," as
in the term *inka shōmei*, the proof of the seal of transmission
that the roshi gives his successor. Ling-yun was confirmed
as a Dharma successor of those peach flowers. Thus with his
creative use of words, his freedom from conceptual baggage, Dogen Zenji clarifies the fundamental location of authority and the true nature of the self. We must obey his
teaching if we are to find our own freedom.

The self is empty and obeys, but what does it obey? You
may say that the self must obey its own light. I would agree,
as would Yun-men. Look again at his teisho on light:

> Yun-men said to his assembly, "Each of you has your own
> light. If you want to see it, you cannot. The darkness is
> dark, dark. Now, what is your light?"
>   Answering for his listeners, he said, "The storeroom!
> The gate!" [8]

The storeroom, the gate, are the sparks that light your
Dharma candle, but they can only be so when you trust
yourself and your setting, as the attendant who answered
Chung Kuo-shih trusted himself. I can imagine a situation
when someone would call and you would remain silent, or
even hide. That too is obedience. You would be responding
truly to the situation, and selflessly you would be saying, in
effect, "I don't belong here."

So it follows that while every place is a dojo, some are
more evidently so. The practice of the self as eternity, joy,
and purity needs a place that is eternal, joyous, and pure.
The Zen Buddhist temple is more reliable in this respect
than a butcher shop. However, it does not get that way just

by architectural design. The sangha of motivated agents of realization creates the true dojo, little by little.

"Dojo" means "place of the Tao," and in this case, "Tao" means enlightenment. The term "dojo" is a translation of "Bodhimanda," the spot under the Bodhi tree where Buddha had his great kensho. He created his Bodhimanda; we create ours.

Moreover, the dojo is a true place of enlightenment without a teacher's presence. In Oregon I visited a dojo that had been established for seven years, and I was the first teacher to go there. But without the sangha, there is only floor, wall, and ceiling, a shell with no creature in it.

The *Heart Sutra* says that the skandhas that make up the self are empty. The dojo is made up of autonomous, empty selves who live by Prajnaparamita and perfectly echo one another. This is obedience in its fundamental implication, and our practice is to realize this implication together.

CHAPTER FIFTEEN

The Search
for the Mind

> P'an-shan gave words of instruction, saying, "In the Three
> Worlds there is no dharma. Where shall we search for the
> mind?" [1]

We can understand the "Three Worlds" in a number of different ways: the worlds of desire, form, and no form; of
greed, hatred, and ignorance; of past, present, and future,
for example. In all of it, as P'an-shan says, there are no dharmas, no phenomena; there is nothing at all to any of it. He
adds, "Where shall we search for the mind?" This is the
koan portion of the case, and shows us how to live in the
emptiness of phenomena, including the self, including the
great mind of the cosmos.

Once Dom Aelred Graham visited Kobori Nanrei Roshi
in Kyoto, in the course of gathering materials for his book,
Conversations: Christian and Buddhist. He showed his host a
calligraphy card on which Alan Watts had inscribed ideographs for the words, "Form is emptiness," and he asked
him to explain the meaning.

Kobori Roshi said, "I don't know the meaning. It is
taken from scripture, a very famous saying." [2]

It seems that Dom Aelred did not get the point, for he changed the subject and went on to talk about the purpose of his visit, which was to illuminate Christianity with insights from Buddhism. But Kobori Roshi had already shot a great bolt of lightning at his earnest guest in direct response to his question. In explaining his need for such light, Dom Aelred did not notice.

Both P'an-shan and the *Heart Sutra* say that form is emptiness. What does that mean? Kobori Roshi said, "I don't know—it's from an old sutra." Is that the meaning?

When the Emperor Wu of Liang asked Bodhidharma, "What is the first principle of the Holy Teaching?" Bodhidharma replied, "Vast emptiness; nothing holy." This is not unlike the response of Jesus to the Roman governor. Pilate asked him, "What is truth?" and Jesus said nothing. This silence is vast and fathomless.

The Emperor pressed Bodhidharma closely and asked, "Who are you, standing here before me?" In other words, "If the Holy Teaching is empty, what are you, in your fine robes, your venerable age, and your distinguished reputation as a Buddhist teacher?"

Bodhidharma replied, "I don't know."[3]

I want to ask you: Is there any difference between Bodhidharma's "I don't know," and Kobori Roshi's "I don't know"? Both I-don't-know's were in response to questions about emptiness.

But where in that emptiness shall we search for the mind? If you imitate Bodhidharma and say, "I don't know," then you are just putting his head on your own. Or if you construct some kind of religious comparison between Bodhidharma and Jesus, you might say something interesting, but it would not be anything that would really help you.

Helping you is the purpose of all this. How can you understand greed, hatred, and ignorance to be vacant? How can you apply this realization? Meister Eckhart writes:

> How can one whose attention is fixed on his loss and misfortune ever be comforted, especially if he keeps visualizing it, brooding over it, his eyes heavy with sorrow, talking to his loss as if they were two persons staring into each other's faces?[4]

Unfortunately, Meister Eckhart then takes a relative position, and says we should cultivate positive thinking. If we have a hundred dollars and lose forty, we should look at the sixty we have left, rather than the forty we have lost. This is not the same as P'an-shan's point, but taken alone and out of context, Meister Eckhart's words about brooding are instructive. We create forms where there are none. How preposterous it is to face a loss! The loss isn't there at all. We are conjuring up a ghost and holding conversation with it.

Realizing that greed, hatred, and ignorance aren't there is a deeper way to resolve them than merely seeking to forget them by looking on the bright side. In Buddhism there are ten kinds of patience, or endurance, and k'ung-jen (ku-nin) is best. This is the endurance of one who reflects on his or her own suffering and knows that it is empty. At this point, endurance becomes a samadhi of frolic and play at the very cliff-edge of birth-and-death.

Lightness and briskness are hallmarks of the realized person, the one who has truly seen through personal suffering, but it is possible to fool oneself into a false state of transparency on the first floor, so to speak, while the basement remains full of cobwebs and rubbish. Zazen is not a quick fix, and realization of a superficial sort is possible without the basement being opened up. Maturity in Buddha's wisdom is a lifetime course, and may require psychological counseling, or at least exposure to frank and friendly advice at certain of its rough spots. It is important to be sensitive to the advice as it comes, for insensitivity to feedback is spiritual pride, the worst of all neuroses, as every true teacher has warned. And throughout, lightness and good humor as practice will help to steer you correctly.

Recently I had occasion to ask a psychiatrist his feelings about feminism. He said, "Feminism is fine if it is not taken too seriously." You may resent this as patronizing, and perhaps in this case his words did have such a flavor. But taken alone, out of the particular context, we can see the truth in the words themselves. Suppose someone were to say, "Women certainly are not equal to men. Can you name a single great female philosopher?" Do you say, "Well, there was Suzanne Langer"? Then for sure there will be a grim argument about the greatness of Suzanne Langer. How much better it is to laugh in his face and say, "Ye Gods, how the human race has suffered from philosophy! You should be glad that women have been wise enough to stay out of it!" The male chauvinist position is ridiculous, hilarious really, and deserves a joke in response, one that will show up the absurdity.

Once in our internment camp, when the war was going badly for the Japanese, the head guard told our camp leader that if Japan lost the war we would all be lined up and shot. On hearing about this, we moped around, feeling very sorry for ourselves indeed. One of the men, an irrepressible clown, came into the room where I was sitting with others, and said in a loud voice, "Hey, did you guys hear the news? The head guard said that if Japan lost the war we would all be lined up and shot."

None of us said anything, but we all fervently wished he would dry up. But he had a point to make. "I tell you, fellows," lowering his voice dramatically, he said, "a hundred years from now it won't make any difference."

We didn't laugh, I am sorry to say. I wonder how we might have reacted if he had said, "Boy, what a great sound that will be, a hundred and seventy-five of us, *bang-bang-bang-bang-bang*!" Perhaps somebody would have throttled him. But really, it would have been a great sound, as a nuclear bomb may be one day.

Recently, Koko An members have been joining the Hawaii Peace Fellowship and other organizations to leaflet the workers and military people at the West Loch gate to Pearl Harbor, where the government stores nuclear weapons. The tone of the leaflets is light and humorous, for indeed humor is essential to realization and communication.

All this relates to our practice in the dojo. Thich Nhat Hanh says you should sit with a half-smile.[5] In the Honolulu Academy of Arts there is a head of a Northern Wei dynasty Buddha on display, wearing a beatific smile. You should all have a look at it. When you are deadly grim about your practice, you place a floor beneath your meditation and you stand firmly there, lifting the weight of your Mu.

True zazen is not like that at all. The bodhimanda of the Buddha is completely empty. This is like a joke—the ordinary structure of things is shattered. Carry your Mu lightly, Nakagawa Sōen Roshi said. When you are light, brisk, and open, you are in touch with the lightness, the briskness, and the openness of self-nature. I remember Kawano Sōkan Roshi saying goodbye to our Bodhidharma figure after his visit with us in Honolulu. He had his suitcase in one hand, and he raised his other hand in a half-*gasshō*, like a mock-military salute, the jauntiest gesture you can imagine.

The monks in Japanese monasteries think they are not supposed to laugh during teisho. They are supposed to be in zazen, listening to the words of the Tathagata. But when Yamamoto Gempo Roshi gave teisho, the assembly was in a shambles of laughter at his stream of jokes, told in his country accent, using peasant images and metaphors that bathed everyone in the essential mud of the rice fields.

In the old days at Koko An, our favorite teisho by Sōen Roshi was case twenty-one of the *Wu-men kuan*, Yun-men's *chien shih chueh*, familiar to Western Zen students in the Japanese rendition, *kanshiketsu*—"dried shit stick." Various euphemistic translations have been offered for kanshiketsu, such as "toilet paper," "dried dirt-wiper," and so on, but the reference is to a stick of soft wood that was used for the same purpose as corncobs that hung in the outhouses of our American ancestors, a hundred years ago.

> A monk asked Yun-men, "What is Buddha?"
> Yun-men said, "Dried shit stick."[6]

Sōen Roshi always made sure his pronunciation did not confuse anybody, for he could not make different sounds for "sit" and "shit." "S-H-I-T," he would spell carefully, "do you understand?" And he would make a graphic gesture below his rear end.

Then he would tell one scatological story after another, including the story about a great teacher in northern Japan who was famous for his marvelous precision of mind and his creative sense of ceremony. One day in the time of greatest cold in winter, his attendant peered into the teacher's *o-benjō*, or "place of convenience," and was most impressed to see a wonderful sculpture of shit, one frozen column and then a single sheet of toilet paper, and another frozen column precisely on top of that, with another single sheet of toilet paper, and so on, rising as a slender tower from the bottom of the pit. A beautiful lesson in benjo ritual.

Sōen Roshi made his point in exactly the same way as Kobori Roshi. He showed the fact itself, divested of all concepts of religion, just as P'an-shan challenges us to do. In this empty universe, where shall we search for the mind?

CHAPTER SIXTEEN

Bringing Forth
the Mind

Don't dwell upon colors to bring forth the mind; don't
dwell upon phenomena of sound, smell, taste, or touch to
bring forth the mind; dwell nowhere and bring forth that
mind.

Diamond Sutra[1]

Clarity for the Buddhist is neither clarity nor confusion,
and therefore, to use the logic found in the *Diamond Sutra*,
it is called clarity. In other words, there is an experience we
call clarity that does not belong in the relative dimension of
clarity, the opposite of confusion. Purity is neither purity
nor stain, and is called purity. The Buddha urges us to bring
forth (literally, give birth to) the clear and pure mind that
does not live upon objects of the senses.

To live upon, to dwell upon, means something other
than gaining sustenance from. Of course we gain sustenance from the objects of our senses: our food, our friends,
our books and records. But what is it that we live upon?
When you look closely, do you find anything there? Though
this is only a preliminary test, the emptiness that the un-
trained person sees with this first glance is the same void of
which the Buddha spoke. But the Buddha spoke from

depths beyond depths of the great empty sea. We make simplistic or absolutist mistakes unless we ourselves find those depths.

How can we deepen? By not dwelling on sense objects, the Buddha tells us. Other teachers tell us the same thing, Meister Eckhart, for example:

> The soul . . . must keep absolutely pure and must live in noble fashion, quite collected and turned inward, not chasing out through the five senses into the multiplicity of creatures.[2]

It is, then, a matter of practice, the cultivation of what Cistercians call "the spirit of silence." "Chasing out through the five senses" is the habit of giving everything a comment: The cat has appeared. The mailman is late. Everything gets a comment when one dwells upon things.

Meister Eckhart says:

> If only you could suddenly be unaware of all things, then you could pass into an oblivion of your own body.[3]

Don't misunderstand: this is not a denial of the body. Many people say that we should get rid of the self; get rid of our desires. But we can be sure that Meister Eckhart had a strong sense of who he was, and that he regularly wanted to eat and sleep. "Suddenly" forgetting the body is, as I read it, "the body and mind fallen away," Dogen Zenji's description of the Great Death.[4] It is at the same time the "fallen-away body and mind," the great preaching career of Meister Eckhart, the marvelous writings of Dogen Zenji, and the act of answering the telephone with complete devotion to the caller—"forgetting the self in the act of uniting with something."[5]

This is zazen, and the daily life of the Zen student. On

your cushions, Mu breathes quietly, and there is no chasing out through the five senses. The forgotten self comes forth, standing up and putting on clothes, and there is still no chasing around.

Bankei Yōtaku Zenji was brought up a Confucian, and as a youth he was puzzled by the Confucian term, "Bright Virtue." He could not find any teacher who could explain it. Finally one teacher suggested that he examine the term in Zen practice. He took up zazen resolutely, almost ruining his health. Finally, as he was sitting in complete silence, the word "unborn" arose in his mind. This was his Bright Virtue. From then on, in a long career, he taught meditation on the unborn, and bringing forth the unborn in daily life. [6]

Meister Eckhart paraphrases a passage from the *Wisdom of Solomon*, "In the midst of silence there was spoken within me a secret word." [7] Theological explanations would have God bringing forth the Son, or Buddha-nature bringing forth realization, but theology has no gut, and can neither sleep nor awaken. Meister Eckhart is referring to human experience.

Yet the silence, the unborn, is not of this world. According to the Gnostic Gospel of Thomas, Jesus said,

> When you make the two one, and when you make the inside like the outside and the outside like the inside, and the above like the below, and when you make the male and the female one and the same . . . . then you will enter [the Kingdom]. [8]

This is the "nowhere" of the *Diamond Sutra*. Using that mind is a matter of living the unborn. It is the unborn, the mind that does not dwell upon phenomena, that experiences the inside and the outside, the above and the below, and the male and the female. Bankei Zenji said:

All of you are facing this way listening to hear me speak, wondering "What will Bankei say?" You are concentrating on listening, and thus none of you has any intention to hear the sound of a crow or a sparrow behind you. The reason you hear things unerringly, and clearly make out various sounds as they occur . . . is because you are listening in accordance with the unborn Buddha-mind.[9]

Listening in accordance with the unborn, building a partition by measuring, cutting, and hammering, focusing only on Mu in zazen, aren't these the acts of bringing forth the mind of nowhere? What is the problem?

The problem is that people do not recognize that the body is the dojo: our mind is the dojo. They suppose that the dojo is a certain room. One bows upon entering and exiting. When we moved the Maui Zendo from its old location, and the old place became the Aitken residence, people still bowed, from habit, on entering what had been the dojo. But every room is a dojo. Watch a Zen monk or nun from Japan who enters your home for the first time. They will hesitate at the threshold, as if bowing.

The problem is that people treat Zen as a hobby. I sense this tendency to some degree in lay Zen centers in Japan, as well as in the West. The atmosphere while doing zazen is vast and fathomless. The atmosphere elsewhere may seem vast, at times, and in certain circumstances, but at other times and places it is altogether limited. Why? This happens when the bow at the entrance to the dojo is just the outer edge of Zen practice.

It is said in Japan that a tea teacher teaches tea even in the bathroom. Dogen Zenji drilled his monks in the practice of zazen at all times. In the bathroom, brushing the teeth, using the toilet, every act is zazen. He composed two gathas for monks to recite before brushing their teeth, one for the attainment of purity, and one to gain teeth strong enough to gnaw through all delusions.[10] Before bathing, monks in all Zen monasteries bow to the floor before the bathroom altar. After the bath, they prostrate themselves again. Before using the toilet, they bow before the underground deity that eats up all their shit, and after using it they bow before him again.

In his instruction to the *tenzō*, or cook of the monastery, Dogen Zenji urges taking care of vegetables and grains to be used for meals "as though they were your own eyeballs." He quoted an old teacher: "When you boil rice, regard the cooking pot as your own head. When you wash rice, know that the water is your own life." He goes on to say:

> If this is not yet clear to you, it is because your thinking runs around like a wild horse and your feeling jumps about like a monkey in a forest. When you let the monkey and horse step back and reflect upon themselves, the oneness of all things is realized naturally. You take a green vegetable leaf and turn it into a sixteen-foot Buddha-body; you take a sixteen-foot Buddha-body and turn it into a green vegetable leaf.[11]

For us lay people living in an industrial, acquisitive society, Dogen Zenji's cautions may seem rather distant and dim—all right for a monastery seven centuries ago, deep in the mountains of Fukui Prefecture, but hardly applicable for people living in the thick of exploitation. How can we help making Zen a kind of hobby when it is so radically different from the world around us?

Our ancestors in the Dharma, with the exception of Vimalakirti, the Layman P'ang, and a few others who hardly do more than prove the rule, did not try to live in the world. Unless we elect to establish monastic regimes, we must find our own way. It seems to me that we have three options:

The first is to establish a career in the arts, in teaching, in a helping profession, or in a business that meets a basic human need, while taking part in the Zendo program, and contributing as much as possible to its leadership, support, and maintenance. This is the Sanun Zendo model, which is well established in Kamakura.

The second is a sangha program of service, based financially on the part-time work of members. This is the Catholic Worker model, and in the Diamond Sangha we see a blending of this model with that of the Sanun Zendo. A number of people are devoting their spare time to sangha publications and to volunteer community work, as well as to helping maintain the temple.

The third is a sangha business, one that is ecologically sound and meets a need in the larger community. It would involve a core group of people who sacrifice more remunerative careers for a creative kind of livelihood that also helps to support the Zendo. Work in the temple garden and on temple maintenance would, of course, be a part of the program. The Zen centers of San Francisco and Los Angeles have experimented with this path.

These possibilities could be combined at a single zendo, but all of them involve a center and a dedicated sangha. It is difficult to follow the Buddha or a religious path of any kind without community. The pressures of our greedy world tend otherwise to drive the sincere individual into isolation —and isolation is death. Even Thoreau had chairs for guests. Robinson Crusoe had to talk with family and friends in his imagination. Your zendo may only be a corner of your bedroom, where you and your spouse sit each morning and evening. Or it may be the living room of your friends, where you go to sit two or three times a week. But without a religious community of some kind, the secular community can take over.

Still, the various options for a religious community are not enough in themselves. They will only turn us into cultists, or back into the mainstream of the Three Poisons, unless we are in touch with the unawareness of Eckhart, with the Buddha's nowhere, with Bodhidharma's vast emptiness, with the oneness of the teachings of Jesus. We must cut off the mind road, so that we are collected, and not chasing out through the five senses.

Not dwelling upon colors, not dwelling on phenomena of sound, smell, taste, and touch, but dwelling in nothing at all, we bring forth that mind. And in a sangha of mutual trust, we find skillful means to bring forth that mind, steadily and steadfastly, in the midst of our poisonous world.

CHAPTER SEVENTEEN

The Mind of Clover

> The Hermit of Lotus Peak held forth his staff before his as-
> sembly and asked, "When the Ancient Ones reached *this*,
> why didn't they stay there?" The assembly was silent.
>
> Answering for his listeners, he said, "Because it has no
> power for guidance." [1]

The original says, "Because it has no power for the path of
others." This case, number twenty-five in the *Blue Cliff Record*, is one of many in our koan study that illustrate the importance of emerging from beneath the Bodhi tree and responding to others.

When the Hermit held forth his staff, what was that?
Just that! Like Fu Ta-shih striking the lectern to expound
the *Diamond Sutra*, [2] the Hermit of Lotus Peak was showing
the Dharma, the pure and clear law-body that comes forth
as all things.

His question was, "When the Ancient Ones attained realization of pure and clear Dharma, why didn't they just
stay in that beautiful place of complete, all-penetrating
peace until they passed on to *parinirvāna*?" When the Buddha was confirmed by the morning star, why did he then

seek out his five disciples? When Mahākāśyapa was confirmed by the Buddha's teaching at Mt. Grdhrakūta, why did he feel compelled to become a teacher himself? And when Dogen Zenji found his body and mind fallen away, why did he bother to return to Japan?

Realizing "just this!" liberated these worthies, freeing them from self-concern and revealing their unity with all beings, but one can't stop there. The fulfillment of your experience of suffering, your com-passion, is a matter of engaging with all beings in their travail.

So the Hermit continues his teisho, still holding out his staff, and asks, "After all, what is it?" Nobody answers, and he says, "Holding my staff across the back of my neck, going to the thousand, the ten thousand peaks."[3] The myriad peaks are not mountains of isolation, but the peaks and valleys of our lives. The Hermit sauntered among these peaks quite at ease with himself, and we can be sure that he guided everyone he met as freely and generously as he guided his assembly in this case.

Our task, too, is to respond generously to others. We can take as our models not only Shakyamuni, the Hermit, and our other great Dharma ancestors, but also such humble beings as bushes and grasses. With every fiber, beings of the plant world are guiding others, perpetuating their species, beginning new species as circumstances permit, conveying their vitality to soil, waters, air, insects, animals, and people. This is Mother Nature, we say in Western culture. This is the *Sambhogakāya*, we say in Buddhism, the body of Indra's Net, the harmony of universal symbiosis. The Sambhogakaya is also our own way of realizing and actualizing that unity.

How do we actualize the oneness of all beings? Through responsibility, the ability to respond—like that of the clover. When the clover is cut, its roots die and release their nitrogen, and the soil is enriched. Earthworms flourish in the rich soil and deposit more nutrients. New seeds fall, take root, mature, and feed other organisms.

Clover does not think about responsibility, and neither did Shakyamuni. He simply arose from his seat and went looking for his friends. The clover simply puts down its roots, and puts up its leaves and flowers.

Fundamentally, the no-thought of the clover and the no-thought of Shakyamuni are the same. They come forth, and their response to circumstances is to give nourishment. No-thought comes forth here as clover, there as Shakyamuni. Single, universal nature appears like this in the world. We identify clover here and Shakyamuni there, and acknowledge that the two are very different indeed. The clover produces pollen for the bees without a thought; Shakyamuni twirls a flower before his assembly without a thought. But clover cannot call a meeting. Shakyamuni cannot metabolize nutrients directly from the soil.

Clover is incapable of not nurturing. It can't do anything but nurture. Shakyamuni is capable of not nurturing. With a poisonous thought, he is a poisonous person. With an enlightened thought, he is an enlightened person. With his great realization, he is unlikely to slip back into poisonous ways, but he could, for he is human.

"All beings are the Tathagata," Shakyamuni said, "but their delusions and attachments keep them from testifying to that fact." What are delusions and attachments? Poisonous thoughts of greed, hatred, and ignorance. The poison of not nurturing. What are enlightened thoughts? Compassionate ones, suffering with others in response to the "sounds of the world."

Shakyamuni went through a metamorphosis from self-centered thinking to enlightenment. This metamorphosis fulfills the possibilities of essential nature in the human being, just as the metamorphosis from caterpillar to butterfly fulfills its possibilities in the Lepidoptera.

What is human metamorphosis? I want to be careful to specify what I mean. With realization, you do not become something else, the way a caterpillar melts inside its cocoon and becomes a butterfly. That kind of analogy creates all kinds of trouble for the Zen student. He or she thinks, "Ah, if only I could have kensho, then all my problems would be solved."

It isn't so. The human being does not metamorphose into something else. Kensho is a peep into essential nature, a glimpse if a shallow experience, a good look if a deeper one. But the practice continues, and in fact it begins there anew.

Nonetheless, the word "metamorphosis" does have some value in describing the Zen process. Truly beginning the practice anew, we learn that somehow we have been victims of our own thinking. We find the original ground that underlies thinking, the source of response. In taking this step, the human being does not become an angel, but rather finds affinity with the silent clover. Our metamorphoses, yours and mine, do not change our form, but rather enable us to acknowledge the ancient truth of no-mind.

All beings, stones, clouds, trees, and animals (including human animals) come forth as no-mind. However, they differ radically in their responsiveness. The clover nurtures itself and its environment without making distinctions. The pig is hostile at some times, friendly at other times. The porpoise rescues the drowning sailor. Where is the human being in this scheme?

Unfulfilled in metamorphosis, the human being is alien, exploiting others by sex, race, class, nation, and species. Fulfilled, we realize and actualize the Net of Indra—with each being nourished by and nourishing all other beings.

The root difference between the exploitive and the nurturing paths is made clear in Dogen Zenji's couplet in the *Genjōkōan*, which I quoted earlier:

> That the self advances and confirms the myriad things is
> called delusion;
> That the myriad things advance and confirm the self is
> enlightenment.[4]

That the nation-state advances and consumes the whole earth with its technology is lethal delusion. That the wilderness of honey-creepers, koa forests, and snowy volcanoes advances and inspires your heart is Buddhahood.

Thus the place of the human being is a matter of choice. We can destroy the gene pool of the earth organism and eliminate all choices, or we can discipline ourselves and find the source of responsibility. That source is the mind of clover. There you are nurtured; there you nurture. Settle there, at least once in your life.

The way is clear in the clover-mind. Self and other are one mind (call it no-mind if you like), the mind of "mountains, rivers, and the great earth, the sun, the moon, and the stars."[5] This is the mind that advances as the song of the cardinal or the scent of incense and confirms the essential self, you and me. This is the mature human experience.

We find here our commonality with the pig at its friendliest and with the porpoise that pushes the exhausted swimmer ashore. We find our commonality with the Buddha preaching to his friends at Vārānasī, and with Gyōgi Bosatsu as he dug waterways for peasants in old Japan.

What, you may ask, about "Nature, red in tooth and claw"? Isn't that also the Tao? What about Blake's "Tiger, tiger, burning bright"? Aren't ferocity and blood-thirst the mind, just like mountains and rivers?

Of course. Universal symbiosis involves the constant absorption of beings by other beings. The bloodstream in your body is such a system in miniature. You may feel that somehow a big tiger is more violent than a little white corpuscle, but essentially both are living out their lives in harmony with the great, dynamic intraplay of the cosmos.

Moreover, we can learn from the tiger. First, for all her violence, the tiger does not threaten the ecosystem as we human beings do. Second, during long periods in her life, the tiger is at rest. She nuzzles her mate, nurtures her cubs, and naps more than other creatures. Now the tiger is violent, now she is at rest.

What is the quality of that rest? She is ready to act, of course, but in that readiness, she is completely relaxed. Reflect upon human rest, as you watch her, lying there so comfortably.

The human being who has not evolved beyond selfishness has no rest. Rather there is something the Buddha called delusion and attachment that permits a continuation of strong feelings. At its extreme, appetite becomes insatiable greed, anger becomes unrelenting hatred, and a weak personal image induces defensive scheming. Most of us are more moderate, but to some degree we all know this constant stream of emotionally charged thinking, and we have no peace, not even in our sleep.

Why should people be afflicted in such a way? This is a key question, one that the Buddha asked. I think that suffering is process. Just as the caterpillar suffers its change, so must we. The same drive that brings the caterpillar out to feed on hibiscus leaves turns it to spinning its cocoon. The same drive that fuels the Three Poisons in the human being matures in realization of mind.

This is the human drive toward peace and unity, but unless it is correctly understood it becomes destructive. If you foolishly seek peace through alcohol, you end up sedating yourself, harming your body, and destroying what peace there may be in your family. If you seek unity in the universe through a multinational corporation, the unity you achieve is your greed with that of many others. The search for peace and unity is correctly the search for realization of the empty, infinite self and the empty, infinite universe—free of concepts, with all things appearing as their own reason.[6]

The long campaign for this realization draws on human racial memory, which in the present stage of evolution is minutely articulate compared to that of other animals. The genes that give humans potential for skills and communication are different from the DNA strands that permit the beaver to build his dam and announce danger with his tail. The beaver must go on making dams in the same way he has done for centuries, but human beings can make dams with more and more refinement in technology.

This sets up problems. We can destroy the earth with our dams. We can annihilate four and a half billion years of earth history with our bombs, and also extinguish the future of the earth, which extends ahead potentially for another almost endlessly long period of time. No other being can do that.

Thus we have a special responsibility to complete the human metamorphoris—to bring the mind of clover to conscious awareness. In touch with that mind, we come forth as mature human beings, realizing that all things are this very self.

Such realization is not wishy-washy. I realize that others are not separate from myself, but if someone very powerful and very reactionary confronts me, I also know very well that he regards me as his antagonist. It is my responsibility to acknowledge his strength within the set we establish and to use it to convey the Dharma, just as a judo expert uses the thrust of his opposite. This is similar to the mondo, the dialogue of Zen teacher and student, and involves a kind of divine cunning in the interaction. The participants are separate individuals, but at the same time they are members of the same nose-hole society, as Nakagawa Sōen Roshi has said.

When the Three Poisons are paramount in our minds, this sense of fundamental kinship is only an abstraction. Recently two men circled the earth for a week at the rate of one circumnavigation every ninety minutes. They encompassed the whole world many times, but they were very high in the air, playing the Marine Hymn and the Air Force Hymn on their hi-fi. In their act of encompassing the world they remained locked in their group, class, and nation—denying the Net of Indra.

Such limited understanding finds its extreme form in the paranoiac who says, "There's a communist in that high-rise spying on me with binoculars." But even people with relatively healthy psyches fall into delusion, and so we scheme about defending ourselves and mastering all beings with our sophisticated intellectual, political, economic, and technological weapons. We advance and confirm the ten thousand things and thus compound delusion and bring the world to an unprecedented crisis.

Like all human institutions, like all humanity and all life and all inanimate things of our world, the Buddha Dharma itself is hostage to our reckless exploitation of the future. There won't be any more Buddha Dharma when our earth is destroyed by nuclear war, or by biological holocaust.

Be clear about this. Distinguish between the Buddha Dharma as Buddhist teachings, and the Dharmakaya as the pure and clear law body. Wu-men wrote, "When the world is destroyed, *it* is not destroyed."[7] "It" is the Dharmakaya, infinite emptiness that is charged with possibilities. It is neither born nor destroyed. Once when I raised the possibility of nuclear annihilation with Yamada Kōun Roshi, he said, "Well, even if the whole earth is utterly destroyed, something, I don't know what, will emerge from essential nature."

This is true, and it is truly an inspiring solace, but in the course of the destruction, the Buddha Dharma, the teachings of the Buddha and all his successors, will be lost. Can you hear Dogen Zenji objecting? I certainly can.

Historically, Zen people nurtured their temples with samu, sutras of work, maintaining buildings and grounds. They supported their religious life with *takuhatsu*, showing the bowl of the Buddha in villages, towns, and cities, while accepting money and food. We have samu and takuhatsu with maintenance work, fund raising, and publications at our Western Zen centers, but maintenance in our present era of great danger means nurturing the temple Earth with the same careful planning we give to our assignments on sangha workdays. Showing the bowl of the Buddha must convey the Dharma, but our unprecedented times demand that it present the Ten Grave Precepts in particular. There is no killing and no stealing in the original mind. When we play games of expedience and compromise, feeding our own ego needs at the expense of others, maintaining our national standards of living at the expense of other countries, then we are neglecting the law of the universe. The universe will find its equilibrium before long.

Coming forth with power for guidance does not mean exactly the same thing for us that it did for the Hermit of Lotus Peak. We have the same responsibility, the same ability to respond, as Bodhisattvas, but our upayas, our compassionate means, will be much different. Today the Buddha Dharma itself must be sprung from its sectarian position to show people everywhere that peace and right action, which they already know in their own hearts, which they learned at mother's breast, is the universal teaching of no-name that can bring decency into our relationships at last.

It follows that Christian, Jewish, Hindu, Moslem, and other faiths must be sprung from their molds also. Traditional Studies, a field pioneered by A. K. Coomaraswamy, Frithjof Schuon, and others, which sets forth perennial metaphysics using metaphors from all world religions, deserves our careful research.[8] There is no such thing as Zen, as we are always being told. That is, there is nothing fixed to be called Zen Buddhism. If so, then there is nothing fixed to be called any particular religion, and we can all learn from each other.

Likewise, there is no closed system to be called psychology, and we can use such psychological devices as sharing meetings and counseling as our own upaya. Western cultural values, such as human equality and reverence for all life, can also be brought into play.

We must save the world, but we can only save it by saving little pieces of it, each of us using his or her own small, partial ability. The task is clear, and very difficult. First we must set about changing our self-centered attitudes as individuals and search out our self-nature under the guidance of a good teacher. Next (the day after we begin to practice, that is) we must set about applying our understanding in the world. This can be overtly a life of service, such as teaching or social work, and it can be service with no tag on it, parenting and working in a store. Finally (on the second day of practice), we need to put our heads and hearts together in synergistic energy to apply the Dharma as a sangha.

I am tired of hearing people say that the application of the teaching is an individual matter. This is the lazy position of someone who does not really take the Bodhisattva vows seriously. If we want to save all beings we can do it efficiently and effectively together, step by step, networking, Indra Networking.

CHAPTER EIGHTEEN

The Morning Star

When the Buddha exclaimed that all beings have the wisdom and virtue of the Tathagata, he had just looked up and noticed the morning star.[1] What connection does Venus in the eastern sky just before dawn have with his pronouncement? What are the implications of that connection for us as Buddhists?

Most people regard Zen practice as a process of purifying the human mind in order to reach a certain condition where a sense experience, such as seeing the morning star or hearing a stone strike a stalk of bamboo, will trigger realization. This process of purifying involves zazen and the rest of the Eightfold Path—right thinking, right action, and so on. When you are ready, some little thing will happen, and then everything will be clear.

It is possible to get such an impression of the Zen process from reading Wu-men's comment on case one of the *Wu-men kuan*. You devote all your energy to Mu, inside and outside become one, and then a single spark lights your Dharma candle.[2] Hakuin Zenji's "Song of Zazen" sets forth the process without mentioning the sense experience. There is a turning about, a fulfillment of your own merit, and you find that singing and dancing are the voice of the Law.[3]

But what is it that turns you about? I suggest that we tend to be self-centered in our attitude toward kensho, and to regard it entirely as the culmination of a human process. We view this process in a psychological way, as though Buddha-nature were coterminous with human nature, and our task is simply to deepen ourselves to the point where we are in touch with our pure essence. Then at that point we are able to acknowledge all kinds of new and interesting things about the universe.

There is enough truth in this self-centered view of the practice to convince the Zen student that it sums up the Buddha Tao. However, it is something like a child's view of procreation. All the facts are in line, but the adult can only smile at the simplistic and mechanical picture they present. The love and the fun and the fulfillment and the mystery are all absent. What is missing in the mechanical view of Zen practice? The star is missing.

What is the star? It is a being, and like other beings it comes forth with the wisdom and virtue of the Tathagata. And like other beings its beauty and mystery are obscured by our self-imposed human limitations. In *The Merchant of Venice*, Lorenzo says to Jessica:

> Look, how the floor of heaven
> Is thick inlaid with patines of bright gold.
> There's not the smallest orb which thou behold'st
> But in his motion like an angel sings,
> Still quiring to the young-ey'd cherubins;
> Such harmony is in immortal souls;
> But whilst this muddy vesture of decay
> Doth grossly close it in, we cannot hear it.
>
> Act V, Scene i

Lorenzo implies that while we are mortal (self-centered?), we cannot hear the harmony of the spheres, but how does he know that? As one of my friends remarked, he obviously does know it, and his lines sing with his knowledge.

When I was eleven and twelve years old, I lived with my grandparents on Mt. Hamilton, where my grandfather was an astronomer at Lick Observatory. On Saturday evenings, the public was invited to drive up from San Jose and nearby areas to look through the two refracting telescopes, the big Thirty-six Inch and the smaller Twelve Inch. On a given Saturday night, the Thirty-six Inch might have been focused on Saturn, and the Twelve Inch on the moon. An astronomer would be on duty to explain scientific matters.

I too would be a part of the viewing public. I would listen carefully to the scientific explanations, but my real motive was to get that brief glimpse through the telescope, of Saturn, or the moon, or some other heavenly body. I never told anybody what happened on those occasions. I don't think I even mused to myself about finding myself out there in space. I only knew that I loved those momentary experiences, and lived for them from week to week.

It was only when I grew up and read Dante that I found that other people also heard music when they looked at the stars. When I found George Meredith referring to stars as "the brain of Heaven," I recalled vividly the awe I felt as a half-grown child looking through the eyepiece of a great telescope aimed at the night sky.[4]

You might say, using Zen language, that I experienced "just that planet," or "just that moon landscape." However, though I was focused on what I was seeing, the experience itself was expansive and liberating. I had a sense of vastness. I lost myself in the universe.

This is a hint of the mature experience of the star, of the flower, of rain on the tin roof. When the Buddha twirled a flower before his assembly, Mahakashyapa smiled. Sometimes in the dokusan room, a student will say that Mahakashyapa experienced just that flower. This is all right as far as it goes, but it doesn't go far enough. Wu-men comments in his verse attached to this case:

> Holding up a flower
> He showed the snake's tail.[5]

Or, as Hsueh-tou said in his introduction to case one of *The Blue Cliff Record*, "When you see horns over a hedge, you know an ox is there."[6] Experiencing the thing in itself, star, flower, tail, horns, is realization of mind. This mind is the myriad things and beings of the universe, and when a single thing advances and confirms the self, all things are realized.

Why is this? "Self nature contains the ten thousand things," as Hui-neng said.[7] Self-nature is your own true nature. It is the great emptiness that is neither inside nor outside, both inside and outside—none other than people, buildings, bushes, animals, birds, and so on.

Confirmed by the morning star, the Buddha found himself in his original home and could acknowledge the fact that all things come forth with the wisdom and virtue of the Tathagata. How do you see Shakyamuni here? What is the wisdom of the Tathagata? Your task as a Zen student is to demythologize the lofty claims for the Buddha's wisdom, and present it as it is, with all its truly miraculous power, as your own body. What is the virtue of the Tathagata? Again, it is important to clarify the marvelous qualities of the Buddha on the verandah of your own house.

Demythologizing does not mean you should reduce your practice to a manipulation of yourself and your environment. The mechanical view of Zen that places the entire function of prajna within the human being is closely related to the self-centered and anthropocentric view of the universe which gives rise to the destruction of the wilderness, the extermination of plant and animal species, the suppression and exploitation of peoples, and the horrible possibilities of nuclear war. When we are preoccupied with ourselves, we are out of touch with things as they are, with the marvels of stars and the grass, and we vent our greed upon the world until our isolation becomes a way of life. Then we can even consider abandoning our earth home and colonizing space, as our ancestors colonized the New World.

When I was a little boy learning to read, I was fascinated by a dreadful book that told the story of the colonization of Australia and Southeast Asia, a book that had been my mother's when she was a little girl. It presented a conventional, bloodthirsty, turn-of-the-century view of the White Man's Burden. There were engravings of natives with fearsome weapons butchering innocent missionaries, and these pictures aroused prurient excitement in me as I pored over them. I can also remember feeling a twinge of sorrow at a picture of English colonists pursuing the natives of Tasmania. I learned either from the text or from my father, who knew about such things, that all the Tasmanian natives were eventually killed off, and that now only people of English and other European extraction live on the island.

I remember thinking that I would not want to live in a place where there were no natives. I was too young to reflect upon the implications of this thought—the fact that I lacked native consciousness and so sought this consciousness in others. I sensed vaguely that when native consciousness is completely eliminated from the land, then everyone is alienated. I did not at that time understand that the traditional people in my own Hawaii were suppressed and exploited, and that many nations in my own United States had been wiped out, while many of the others had been reduced to an ultimate kind of indignity.

We residents of Hawaii and North America live in a kind of space colony because we cannot acknowledge the star, the *hila-hila* grass, or the deer. We have forgotten (if we ever knew them) the teachings of the Peacemaker, revered as founder of the Iroquois Confederacy, and the traditions within which he arose:

> We are shown that our life exists with the tree life, that our well-being depends on the well-being of the vegetable life, that we are close relatives of the four-legged beings. In our ways, spiritual consciousness is the highest form of politics. . . . We believe that all living things are spiritual beings. Spirits can be expressed as energy forms manifested in matter. A blade of grass is an energy form manifested in matter—grass matter. The spirit of the grass is that unseen force which produces the species of grass, and it is manifest to us in the form of real grass.[8]

This passage is part of the "Haudenosaunee Address to the Western World," presented to the United Nations at Geneva in 1977, and is startlingly similar to the Buddhist position. In Dogen Zenji's writings we read that all existences are Buddha nature, and in Yamada Roshi's teishos we hear the same fact from the opposite perspective, that Buddha-nature is empty infinity that is full of possibilities.

Notice that the Haudenosaunee statement begins with the words, "We are shown." How are we shown? By the grass itself, by the star itself. Of course the Native American has ways to prepare for such an experience. As Zen Buddhists we have zazen, dokusan, teisho, and the life of the precepts. Learning concentration and cultivating sensitivity to experience is profoundly important. But the experience itself is not merely an isolated act of personal human adjustment. After zazen we should step out and look up at the sky.

Dogen Zenji makes this process clear in a celebrated passage in his *Genjokoan*:

> To study the Buddha-way is to study the self.
> To study the self is to forget the self.
> To forget the self is to be enlightened by the ten thousand
>   dharmas.[9]

For "dharmas" in this case, read "phenomena." It is the myriad things of the universe that confirm you and me. The fundamental substance is Buddha-nature. Native Americans use the term "Good Mind" for what they perceive to be fundamental. For both Buddhists and Native Americans, essential nature pervades all phenomena, here with the energy form to be a blade of grass, there with the energy form to be a star.

The Native American finds oneness with the world through fasting, isolation, and dreams. The Zen student sits in the Zen hall practicing concentration and serenity. Differences between the two paths and their expressions are clear and distinct. But both acknowledge the experience of the myriad things advancing and confirming the human self.

Modern Native Americans have built on their tradition and can acknowledge that spiritual consciousness is the highest form of politics. Modern Zen Buddhists are only beginning to move outside their monastery walls to acknowledge the social power of their convictions. In this process, we Buddhists can learn from the Peacemaker:

> "Righteousness" refers to something akin to the shared ideology of the people using their purest and most unselfish minds. It occurs when the people put their minds and emo-

tions in harmony with the flow of the universe and the intentions of the Good Mind. . . . The principles of Righteousness demand that all thoughts of prejudice, privilege,
or superiority be swept away and that recognition be given
to the reality that the creation is intended for the benefit of
all equally . . . the birds and animals, the trees and the insects, as well as the humans.[10]

This is a part of a summary of the Peacemaker's principles
that forms the Constitution of the Iroquois Confederation.
I am reminded of the admonitions on the subject of equality
that Yamada Roshi often repeats to us: we must rid ourselves of invidious concepts of high and low, sage and ordinary person, male and female.

I am reminded of Gary Snyder's words in "Buddhism and
the Coming Revolution":

Avatamsaka [Hua-yen] Buddhist philosophy sees the
world as a vast interrelated network in which all objects and
creatures are necessary and illuminated. From one standpoint, governments, wars, or all that we consider "evil" are
uncompromisingly contained in this totalistic realm. The
hawk, the swoop, and the hare are one. From the "human"
standpoint we cannot live in those terms unless all beings
see with the same enlightened eye. The Bodhisattva lives
by the sufferer's standard, and . . . must be effective in aid-
ing those who suffer.[11]

Gary Snyder goes on to point out that the "mercy of the
West has been social revolution; the mercy of the East has
been individual insight into the basic self/void," and adds,
"We need both." Indeed. We need also the teaching of
science, for example the wisdom of Lewis Thomas, who
makes it clear that all of us, trees, waters, animals, people,
worms, and nettles are intimately interconnected in universal symbiosis.

Nothing is static, and today we face the possibility that we live in the end-time. We seem to be carried along by mass karma, yet I believe that it will only take a single leap in consciousness for the human race to change its dangerously exploitive ways. One individual life of integrity reminds us all that truth is the only possible Tao. One small group of people truly dedicated to reinhabiting the earth with native, enlightened consciousness can convince the nations.

We have the human talent of Shakyamuni, of the Peacemaker, and of the patriarchs and matriarchs in the past who have been shown by a star, by a coyote, or by a shout in the sacred hall that "the earth and I are of one mind," as Chief Joseph has said. [12] All of us hold in our hearts the archetype of hard practice and its application, the Tao of Samantabhadra, the Bodhisattva of Great Action. Let us put our minds and emotions together in righteousness.

CHAPTER NINETEEN

The Way
and Its Virtue

The purpose of Zen practice is the perfection of character.

Yamada Kōun Roshi

Many people shy away from the idea of "perfection." They know that "nobody is perfect" and so they neglect their own characters and don't try to correct themselves. Other people tend to be perfectionistic and are reinforced in their neuroses by moral teaching. And there is the question posed by the young Dogen, "If all beings are Buddha, why all this striving?" [1] "Perfection" seems to open a can of worms.

Yet it is a term that can open the true way. The one who knows that nobody is perfect can also afford to be aware of personal failings without being discouraged by them. The one who is moderately perfectionistic has a well developed conscience and is prepared to do zazen. The one who knows that all beings by nature are Buddha is not always looking to the future, but seeks true nature in this moment.

Yamada Roshi is showing us how to reveal the essence in ourselves and in the world. He sums up the Six *Pāramitās* or "Perfections" of classical Buddhism with the term "perfection of character." To understand his succinct dictum clearly, it is useful to examine these six perfections in detail. They are: relinquishment, morality, equanimity, vigor, meditation, and realization.

Relinquishment or dana is the letting go, or cutting off, of greed, hatred, and ignorance, the Three Poisons. Many translators render the Paramita of Relinquishment as the "Perfection of Charity." This is all right so long as you understand "charity" in the Pauline sense: "The greatest of these is charity."[2] In fact, in that dimension, "charity" is a richer word than "relinquishment" for it evokes the caritas of sharing, the affective dimension of love.

This is an example of how religions may enhance one another. "Letting go" tends to get austere; "charity" tends to get mushy. The Danaparamita can become the Middle Way.

Morality in classical Buddhism is the observance of the precepts, not killing, not stealing, not misusing sex, not lying, not clouding the mind, and so on. Precepts are useful for the Zen student, who seeks to internalize them, to find their source in the mind, and to make morality altogether familiar.

Moral behavior that is altogether familiar is the mark of the truly mature person. Everyone else needs guidelines, and given the Zen proverb, "Shakyamuni Buddha is only half-way there," we can all take the precepts as refreshing reminders.

Equanimity is the condition where you are not thrown off balance by anything. It is not endurance, and at the same time it is not apathy. If, for example, your spouse is unfaithful, you will naturally become troubled. The trust you have established is violated; the family you have formed is disrupted. But even in the agony of betrayal, the great mind is completely steady, like the depths of the ocean in a storm. Dwelling there, you can take the action and make the statements that may be required to help save everyone concerned, including yourself.

Sometimes you can be in touch with the great mind in a crisis, but neglect it at less significant junctures. Equanimity is also a matter of graciously accepting minor criticism. Often the so-called little things are more of a challenge than dramatic threats.

Vigor is the act coming forth unself-consciously, in keeping with circumstances, unfettered by any conceptual attachments—even to "love" or "justice." "Dwell nowhere, and bring forth that mind."[3] This is the way of Great Action.

Vigor is not blind, however; it is not mere spontaneity. Be careful on this point. The maniac shooting his family is also unself-conscious. In fact, he is unconscious, because he has lost his human nature. He is a victim who creates victims, a stark contrast to the selfless Bodhisattva, who is suffering with the other.

Meditation is zazen, the human mind rigorously focused and quiet. The Sanskrit term is *Dhyānapāramitā*, and the model for *dhyāna* is the figure of the Buddha, seated erect and cross-legged, fully alert, and entirely at rest.

Dhyana is also the mindful spirit of the Zen student in daily life. "Attention" is the watchword of Zen. Every parent tells her child, "Mind what you are doing." Good advice for adults as well.

Realization is confirmation of the self by the mourning dove, by the tinkle of a teacup shattering, by the laugh of a friend. It is the acknowledgment of the interpenetration and intercontainment of all things, beginning with yourself, and of their empty infinity in the vast and fathomless universe. This is the Prajnaparamita, the Perfection of Wisdom.

All Buddhists speak of realization, but they may mean different things. To mention only a few: for the Theravada Buddhist, it brings understanding that all life is ephemeral. For the Mahayana Buddhist, it clarifies the empty Net of Indra, but some Mahayana schools declare that such clarification is only for Shakyamuni Buddha and perhaps a few others, or that it comes to the individual after death. Zen and some streams of the esoteric tradition take realization as a personal possibility. In fact, for the Zen student, all Six Paramitas are qualities to be perfected as the self.

The Chinese word *te* and its equivalent in Japanese, *toku*, sum up the Six Paramitas. We encounter it frequently in our Zen study; for example, in the *Heart Sutra* we read, "*Mu chi yaku mu toku*," that is, in the Prajnaparamita there is "no wisdom and no attainment."[4] "Attainment" is one translation of *te* or *toku*, "virtue" is another. Both have their strengths and weaknesses in rendering the original. I want to use the word "virtue" for our purposes, despite the sentimental overtones it has for some people. It is indeed virtue that we try to uncover in our practice.

At the same time, "virtue," "the Six Paramitas," "perfection of character"—these are simply labels for an organic process. Breathing in and out, you let go of poisons and establish the serene ground of the precepts. You release defenses of the self and the mind comes forth boldly with the count of "one," "two," "three." Focused and serene, you are ready for instruction by the ten thousand things.

The practice of virtue is set forth in the *Tao Te Ching*, known in Japan as the *Dōtokukyō* (*The Book of the Way and Its Virtue*), the central text of Taoism, which could also be called Te-ism, for *Te* receives as much attention as *Tao*:

> To obtain trust, put your trust in others.
> Take care! Speak only when it is essential.

Then when your work is done and the job is finished,
Everyone will say that it happened naturally.[5]

Thus, in the world, too, there is nothing to be called virtue. I remember visiting with Suzuki Shunryū Roshi in his study at the Zen Center of San Francisco. He said, "I don't do anything. I just sit here and the members organize themselves and buy the Page Street building and set it up as a zendo. They buy the Tassajara Hot Springs Resort and establish it as a mountain retreat. It is not my doing."

Then how did it happen? Obviously something was operating. Long ago, I met an older Japanese man in Honolulu who had spent eight years as a monk at the Rinzai monastery Myōshinji in Kyoto. After he came to Hawaii, he was a Japanese school teacher for a while, then a priest, and when I knew him he was a businessman. He wanted very much to organize a Zen center, but it never worked out. He said, "I have no toku."

His honesty was moving and endearing, but I must say that his "no toku" and Suzuki Roshi's "no toku" were different, for their practice was different. When your practice is to reveal the essence, you are teaching without overtly teaching. You forget yourself and trust others, in effect revealing to them their own essence, and they themselves turn the Dharma wheel.

CHAPTER TWENTY

Religious Activism
and the Tao

Activism is of two kinds, generally speaking. The first is organized effort to expose and correct particular social evils or dangers, such as excessive profit taking or pollution of the environment. This is watchdog or gadfly liberalism, which seeks to keep the conventional system in order.

The second kind of social activism is millenarianism, the search for and the realization of the Kingdom of God, by whatever name, in this world. This involves a philosophical rejection of the acquisitive ways of society, and a "return" to the values of equality and compassion.

Sometimes the millenarian will take on the coloration of a reformer, as when a Catholic Worker joins in a movement to boycott a harmful commercial product. Sometimes reformers may seem utopian in their resistance to social evils on many fronts.

The difference is one of attitude toward the issues. For one in search of the Kingdom of God, the issue is a symptom; for the reformer, the issue is the disease. For, say, Daniel Berrigan, the war in Vietnam was a symptom of a corrupt social and economic system. For, say, Eugene Mc-

Carthy, it was an aberration or growth upon an otherwise generally acceptable system.

The search for the Kingdom of God is religious, although sometimes formal religion is rejected. The historical roots of the search extend back through the New Testament to the prophetic writings of Judaism. Moreover, the faith of such humanist movements as Marxism and philosophical anarchism in "eternal principles" make them religious despite their protests to the contrary.

Early Christians resisted Roman repression, and when the Church became accepted politically, resistance movements that practiced communal living, poverty, and sharing, split off from the main stream of the organized religion, beginning with the Montanists in the second century, and continuing through the Brethren of the Free Spirit in Germany, the Ranters in England, through the Friends and the Mennonites to the Catholic Workers and the Amish in the United States today.[1] These movements have interpreted the words of Jesus, "Seek ye first the Kingdom of God," more concretely than most theologians.

Where is the Kingdom of God? Your answer may depend upon what text you read. In the *Jerusalem Bible*, widely accepted among modern Catholics, you will find Jesus saying, in Luke 17:20, "The Kingdom of God is among you."[2] This seems to mean that the Kingdom is actualized when people gather together as the Church.[3]

The King James translation of the words of Jesus, "The Kingdom of God is within you," implies a theology of immanence, which, as Joseph Campbell observes, "is exactly what the Church, following the footsteps of the prophets, has been condemning as heresy these many centuries."[4]

From Nag Hammadi we find the Gnostic reading to be different again. At the end of the "Gospel of Thomas," in a context very similar to the passage in Luke, Jesus says, "The Kingdom of the Father is spread out upon the earth and men do not see it."[5]

This version brings harmony to the polarizations of "among" and "within," and neatly handles the problem of evil. The Kingdom is like a film that overlies all things, including one's self. We can't see it, and so we may be evil despite the goodness that covers us. The problem of evil is thus a problem of ignorance, as it is in Buddhism.

The millenium in Buddhism is variously called Nirvana, the Lotus Land, and the Pure Land. Hakuin Zenji expresses vividly the Buddhist conviction that the Kingdom and the everyday world are one and the same:

> This very place is the Lotus Land;
> this very body the Buddha.[6]

Nothing is overlaid—the Kingdom is both inside and outside; neither inside nor outside. We don't realize this fact, however.

> How sad that people ignore the near,
> and search for truth afar;
> like someone in the midst of water
> crying out in thirst;
> like a child of a wealthy home
> wandering among the poor.[7]

Hakuin Zenji says, in effect, "Heaven is here and we are God, but we don't realize that fact." Thus we live selfishly and create poverty, exterminate Jews, and bomb innocent peasants; we drug ourselves with chemicals and television, and curse our fate when the cancer of human waste appears in our own precious bodies. We ignore the near, the intimate fact that heaven lies about us in our maturity, and thus we cannot apply any of its virtues.

Hakuin's experience showed him that nirvana is samsara, the absolute is the relative, the timeless world is the world of ends and means. In Western tradition we must search out prophetic Christians to find expressions of the absolute as the relative:

> To see a World in a Grain of Sand
> And a Heaven in a Wild Flower,
> Hold Infinity in the palm of your hand
> And Eternity in an hour.[8]

And the lesson is difficult for Asians also. As I indicated earlier, when Dogen Zenji was a young monk, he was greatly troubled by the apparent contradiction between the Buddhist tradition that all beings are enlightened as they are, and the fact that every greatly enlightened teacher in Buddhist history had to devote many arduous years to becoming enlightened.[9] Christianity would have much the same problem if it could be shown that Jesus meant simply to say, "You are God." What about sin? What about the labor of the saints to see God? Actually, as I understand it, he indicated that we are meant to be *as* God, made in his image. "Be ye perfect, even as your Father in heaven is perfect."[10]

When the Buddha said, "All beings are the Tathagata," he went on to say, "Only their delusions and attachments keep them from realizing that fact."[11] "The whole universe groans and travails" awaiting glorification.[12] It is important for Buddhists to balance the two sides of the proposition.

We are all right from the very beginning, but this is not something readily apparent until we have rooted out our ego-concerns and our relativistic views. To say that I'm okay and you're okay without showing how self-preoccupation interferes with realization is heresy, just as clearly as

"You are God" in a simple dualistic context would be mistaken. Hakuin's lines about this very place and body are found in his poem called, "Song of Zazen"—that is, "Song of Meditation." Meditation, correctly practiced, is the way the Buddha and his followers have used to realize the fact that practice is itself enlightenment, this very body is essential nature, and the Kingdom is not far away.

Here and there in Buddhist history we find millenarian individuals devoting themselves to social welfare and social protest, but generally the practice of enlightenment, social or individual, was focused within the monastery and among monks. We do not find Buddhist social movements developing until the late nineteenth century, under the influence of Christianity and Western ideas generally. Gandhi was influenced both by Buddhism and his native Hinduism, but he probably could not have developed his Satyagraha philosophy of social action without having read the New Testament and the writings of Tolstoy and Thoreau.

In the West we find millenarian movements preoccupied with ends and means—in the case of the Crusades, the placement of "Jerusalem" in a foreign country to be taken in future time. The Brethren of the Free Spirit resorted to violence, even murder, in their efforts to find peace and freedom. Though in our own time we have the saying attributed to A. J. Muste, "There is no way to peace; peace is the way," I doubt if this could have been formulated without the influence of Gandhi, who showed that *swaraj*, or independence, is right here now, not some time in the future, when he made salt beneath the truncheons of the British Raj.

"Right here now," "Peace is the way," "This very body is the Buddha," "The Kingdom of God is within you"— these are all expressions of human intimacy with essential nature, which is not born and does not die. In Chinese Buddhist texts, the word "intimacy" is a synonym for kensho, seeing into true nature, consciously experiencing true nature. Often a classical dialogue will end: "And the monk became enlightened." Sometimes it will end, "And the monk became intimate." The meaning is the same.

What is the opposite of intimacy? It is self-consciousness, first of all. I cannot be intimate with you if I am preoccupied with myself. With self-preoccupation comes abstraction from experience, and conceptual thought. Meister Eckhart warns us over and over against self-conscious abstraction:

> When . . . the soul is aware that it is looking at God, loving him, and knowing him, that is already a retrogression.[13]

The Kingdom of God is the Kingdom of Peace, but we are not peaceful because in our self-consciousness we are preoccupied with what we think we are and what we think we are doing. The pale cast of conceptual thought obscures our true life. Wu-men wrote:

> With a bit of *has* or *has not*
> body is lost! Life is lost![14]

Don't misunderstand. I am not saying that concepts are no good. Concepts are there to be used. It is important to conceptualize about peace. We fall into error when we permit concepts to use us. How can we wipe away fixed ideas of "has" and "has not"? The problem is not in the cortex. Our brain secretes thoughts as our stomach secretes pepsin. The real question is, how would you show the Kingdom of God in your own ephemeral circumstances?

I would say, "Please pass the pepper." Do you think I am being facetious? If so, perhaps you are still self-conscious.

When you, a person who lives and dies, holds infinity in the palm of your hand, you tangle eyebrows with Hakuin and identify the Lotus Land correctly. The crusaders slaughtered people and were themselves slaughtered in attempting to take Jerusalem from the infidels. That's heresy. Jerusalem was right there at home—how sad that they searched afar!

William Blake wanted to build Jerusalem in England's green and pleasant land, but Wu-men would have checked him closely. Here is Blake's stanza in full:

> I will not cease from Mental Fight,
> Nor shall the Sword sleep in my hand
> Till we have built Jerusalem
> In England's green and pleasant Land. [15]

What would Wu-men have said? Perhaps he would have asked, "What is Jerusalem?" How would Blake have responded? Could he have gestured at his crowded studio and said, "Here it is!"?

As Gandhi showed us, the practice of the Kingdom of God, which he called "the light," is sometimes the practice of Mary at the feet of Jesus, and sometimes that of Martha serving up the soup. It may sometimes be very active indeed.

For Jesus, at one point, the Kingdom of God meant cleansing the temple of money-changers. Hakuin said, "This very body is the Buddha," and he took the lord of his province to task for the economic plight of the peasants.

One of my colleagues has said that we should embrace the bomb. He means, I think, that the bomb is part of our karma. It is not "out there." I agree, but I would not say it in such a way.

When a child wanders into a busy city intersection, that is no time to rhapsodize about the law of karma or the will of God. No: anybody with any gumption will snatch that child from the wheels of oncoming taxis and trucks. How does the person of gumption deal with the bomb?

As Gandhi said, we must follow our own light. We learn from Gandhi's life that the light is informed by religious tradition. We learn something more precise from Yunmen: the light is not simply an inner matter. The storeroom and gate instruct us.

What is my light? Where is my light?

CHAPTER TWENTY-ONE

Gandhi, Dōgen, and Deep Ecology

> A friend once inquired if Gandhi's aim in settling in the village and serving the villagers as best he could were purely humanitarian. Gandhi replied. . . . "I am here to serve no one else but myself, to find my own self-realization through the service of these village folk." [1]

This remarkable conversation reveals Gandhi's stature as a world teacher. It is a true mondo, with the enlightened one responding to the fixed attitude of the questioner, turning the question around and using it as a vehicle for showing the truth that the question in its original form actually obscured.

The question was asked, not without malice, from the conventional suspicion of generosity: Isn't everything you do for others really a way of aggrandizing yourself? Is there really such a thing as pure generosity? Is it possible to live just for others? Aren't you serving your own psychological needs by living with poor people like this?

Gandhi replied from a point of view that is not conventional. He omits the word "humanitarian" entirely from his reply, and indeed I wonder if it is found anywhere in his writings or speeches. For the questioner, humanitarianism seems unrealistic, and in effect, Gandhi acknowledges this, agreeing in order to make a deeper point.

Like a judo expert, Gandhi uses the energy and thrust of the other. Challenged to deny that he is just serving himself, he does not deny it at all, but takes the challenge a step further, and states clearly that the villagers are serving him.

This is not self-aggrandizement, but the way of self-realization, as Gandhi says. Ego-concerns vanish, and the true nature of the one who observes and takes action becomes clear. It is none other than all beings and all things. Thomas Merton observes that Gandhi's practice was the awakening of India and of the world within himself[2]—or, I would say, as himself. Merton obviously felt this was an existential awakening, but whether it was existential or merely political, the truth remains: the other is no other than myself.

The conventional view that serving others is a means for self-aggrandizement is the view that accepts exploitation of people and the environment, wars between nations, and conflicts within the family. As Yasutani Roshi used to say, the fundamental delusion of humanity is to suppose that I am here and you are out there.

Gandhi's view is traditionally Eastern, and is found with differing emphases in Hinduism, Taoism, and in Theravada and Mahayana Buddhism. For Dogen Zenji and for Zen Buddhists generally, the way is openness to all beings, all things. Each being confirms my self-nature, but if I seek to control the other, I fall into delusion. The *Genjokoan* again:

> That the self advances and confirms the myriad things is called delusion.
> That the myriad things advance and confirm the self is enlightenment.[3]

The self imposing upon the other is not only something called delusion, it is the ruination of our planet and all of its creatures. But enlightenment is not just a matter of learning from another human being. When the self is forgotten, it is recreated again and again, ever more richly, by the myriad things and beings of the universe:

> The wild deer, wand'ring here & there
> Keeps the Human Soul from Care.[4]

This is not just a matter of sensing the oneness of the universe. Stars of a tropical sky spread across the ceiling of my mind, and the cool wind unlocks my ear.

Such experiences are not philosophy and are not confined to the traditional East, but in the past two hundred years, East or West, we must look to the periphery of culture, rather than to the mainstream, to find anything similar. The mainstream follows a utilitarian interpretation of God's instructions to Noah:

> And the fear of you and the dread of you shall be upon every beast of the earth, and upon every fowl of the air, and upon all that moveth on the earth, and upon all the fishes of the sea; into your hand they are delivered.[5]

It is only a very few, relatively isolated geniuses in the West, such as Wordsworth and Thoreau, who have taught confirmation of the human self by nature, and the crime of confirming nature by the self. For example, here Wordsworth echoes Dogen:

> Think you, 'mid all this mighty sum
> Of things for ever speaking,
> That nothing of itself will come,
> But we must still be seeking?[6]

Openness to the myriad things follows what George Sessions, in his discussion of deep ecology, calls conversion:

> The forester ecologist Aldo Leopold underwent a dramatic conversion from the "stewardship" shallow ecology re-

source-management mentality of man-over-nature to announce that humans should see themselves realistically as "plain members" of the biotic community. After the conversion, Leopold saw steadily and with "shining clarity" as he broke through the anthropocentric illusions of his time and began "thinking like a mountain."[7]

Man-over-nature is the self advancing and confirming the myriad things, an anthropocentric delusion. It is the same mind-set as Americans over Vietnamese, or men over women, or managers over workers, or whites over blacks.

The Deep Ecology movement has grown out of the despair of ecologists over the conventional resource-management mentality that is rapidly depleting our minerals, razing our forests, and poisoning our rivers and lakes. It is precisely the same as the welfare society mentality that manages human resources for the short-term benefit of the managers themselves.

Readers of the conventional media have more awareness of the dangers of war and nuclear poison than they have of the biological holocaust involved in clearing jungles, strip-mining mountains, disrupting the balance of life in oceans, and draining coastal swamps. One must read the journals and bulletins of ecological societies to gain a perspective of the accelerating global disaster that our luxurious way of life is bringing down upon us all.

But even with knowledge, I wonder if it would be possible to reverse the machine of death and destruction. We in the peace movement have sought to levitate the Pentagon, falling into the same delusion that Dogen Zenji warns us about. When we stopped the B–1 Bomber, we got the Cruise Missile. When we stopped the Omnibus Crime Bill, we got another Omnibus Crime Bill. When we stopped LBJ, we got Richard Nixon.

The point is that, with all our good intentions, we are

still seeking to advance and control the myriad things. The alternative is not just to respond passively or to run away. Once one thinks like a mountain, the whole world is converted. All things confirm me. Then I sit on dojo cushions that do not move. There is no controller and no one to control.

I think again of Gandhi, urging each of us to follow our own light. Erik H. Erikson suggests that Gandhi held fast to his values to the exclusion of human needs in his family and even in his nation.[8] Probably so. We need not venerate him blindly. With all his flaws, he was surely a forerunner of a New Reformation that seeks to encourage self-sufficiency and personal responsibility for all beings and all things.

In the Buddhist world we have in the past generation seen the development of Sarvodaya Shramana in Sri Lanka, the Coordinating Group for Religion in Society in Thailand, the School of Youth for Social Service in South Vietnam, and Ittōen in Japan. These movements developed in the modern zeitgeist of social consciousness, and have found guidance in the Buddhist doctrine of non-ego and in the Buddhist precepts, just as Gandhi could find guidance for the Indian independence movement in the ancient Hindu doctrine of self-reliance.

In the Christian world, we have seen the rise of similar movements, notably the Catholic Worker, an anarchist network of communal houses in dozens of American cities, set up by families of laymen and laywomen to feed the poor, clothe them, and shelter them, just as Jesus taught: "Inasmuch as you have done it to one of the least of these my brothers and sisters, you have done it to me."[9]

These movements grew from their roots with the understanding that confirmation by the myriad things is not just an esoteric experience confined within monastery walls. Swaraj, or independence, was for Gandhi the self-reliance of individuals who practiced the way of realization by complete openness to the British, the ultimate "other" for colonial India. It is also, as Gandhi indicated to the one who questioned his humanitarianism, the practice of being with the poor, the handicapped, the oppressed, thinking as they do, drawing water and digging the earth as they do. It is the practice of realization through their service—and through the service of all others, including police and politicians.

The practice of "being with them" converts the third person, *they*, *it*, *she*, *he*, into the first person, *I* and *we*. For Dogen Zenji, the others who are "none other than myself" include mountains, rivers, and the great earth. When one thinks like a mountain, one thinks also like the black bear, and this is a step beyond Gandhi's usual concerns to deep ecology, which requires openness to the black bear, becoming truly intimate with him.

This is compassion, suffering with others. Look again at the *Diamond Sutra*: "Dwell nowhere, and bring forth that mind." "Nowhere" is the zero of purest experience, known inwardly as peace and rest. To "come forth" is to stand firmly and contain the myriad things. For the peace or ecology worker, the message of the *Diamond Sutra* would be: "From that place of fundamental peace, come forth as a man or woman of peace, presenting peace in the inmost community of those who would destroy it."

APPENDIX

The Diamond Sangha Ceremony on the Death of an Unborn Child

1. Three full bows.
2. *Vandana* and *Ti Sarana* in Pali, or *Taking Refuge* in English.
3. *Enmei Jikku Kannon Gyo*, or other short sutra in Japanese or English.
4. Leader:

We gather today to express our love and support for _____
_____, and for _____ [names of parents], and to say farewell to a child unborn, a bit of being we have named _____, who appeared just as we all do, from the undifferentiated mind, as that mind, and who passed away after a few moments of flickering life, just as we all do.

In our culture, we place great emphasis upon maintaining life, but truly death is not a fundamental matter, but an incident, another wave. Bassui Zenji speaks of it as clouds fading in the sky. Mind essence, Bassui says, is not subject to birth or death. It is neither being nor nothingness, neither emptiness nor form and color.

It is, as Yamada Kōun Roshi has said, infinite emptiness, full of possibilities, at once altogether at rest and also charged with countless tendencies awaiting the fullness of karma. Here _____ is in complete repose, at one with the mystery that is our own birth and death, our own no-birth and no-death.

5. *Heart Sutra* in Japanese or English, as parents, leader, and
   friends offer incense.
6. Leader:
   Buddha nature pervades the whole universe,
   existing right here now;
   with our reciting of Enmei Jikku Kannon Gyo
   and the Great Prajnaparamita Heart Sutra
   let us unite with
   the Ancient Seven Buddhas,
   Fully Realized Shakyamuni Buddha,
   Great Compassion Avalokiteshvara Bodhisattva,
   Earth Treasury Ksitigarbha Bodhisattva,
   all Founding Teachers, past, present, future.

   We especially dedicate our love and our prayerful
      thoughts to you _____.
   may you rest in perfect peace.

   Let true Dharma continue—
   Sangha relations become complete.
   All:
   All Buddhas throughout space and time,
   all Bodhisattvas, Mahasattvas,
   the Great Prajnaparamita.
7. *Great Vows for All* in English.
8. Three full bows.

A Table of
Chinese-Japanese Equivalents

NAMES AND BOOK TITLES

Chinese (Wade-Giles)	*Japanese*
Ch'ang-ch'ing	Chōkei
Ch'ang-sha	Chōsa
Chao-chou	Jōshū
Cheng-tao ko	*Shōdōka*
Chiang-nan	Kōnan
Chien-yuan	Zengen
Ching-ch'ing	Kyōsei
Chung Kuo-shih	Chū Kokushi
Fa-yen	Hōgen
Feng-hsüeh	Fuketsu
Fu Ta-shih	Fu Daishi
Hsin-hsin ming	*Shinjinmei*
Hsiu-shan	Shūzan
Hsüeh-feng	Seppō
Hsüeh-tou	Setchō
Hua-yen	*Kegon*
Hui	E
Hui-hai	Ekai
Hui-neng	Enō

NAMES AND BOOK TITLES

Chinese (Wade-Giles)	*Japanese*
Hung-jen	Gunin
Jui-yen	Zuigan
Kuei-shan	Isan
Ling-yün	Reiun
Ma-tsu	Baso
Mu-chou	Bokushū
Nan-ch'üan	Nansen
Pai-chang	Hyakujō
P'an-shan	Banzan
P'ang	Hō
Pao-fu	Hōfuku
Shih-shuang	Sekisō
Tan-hsia	Tanka
Tao-wu	Dōgo
Te-shan	Tokusan
Ti-tsang	Jizō
Ts'ai-ken t'an	*Saikontan*
Ts'ui-yen	Suigan
Wu *of* Liang	Bu *of* Ryō
Wu-men	Mumon
Wu-men kuan	*Mumonkan*
Wu-tsu	Goso
Yang-shan	Kyōzan
Yen-t'ou	Gantō
Yüan-wu	Engo
Yüeh-shan	Yakusan
Yün-men	Unmon
Yün-yen	Ungan

Notes

THE NATURE OF THE PRECEPTS

1. See Irving Babbitt, trans., *The Dhammapada* (New York: New Directions, 1965), p. 30.
2. D. T. Suzuki, *Zen and Japanese Culture* (New York: Pantheon, 1959), pp. 114–115.
3. Takuan Zenji echoes Krishna's advice to Arjuna:

> These bodies are perishable, but the dwellers in these bodies are eternal, indestructible, and impenetrable. Therefore fight, O descendant of Bharata!
>
> He who considers this (Self) as a slayer or he who thinks that this (Self) is slain, neither of these knows the Truth. For It does not slay, nor is It slain.
>
> "Bhavagad Gita," II, 17–19
> Lin Yutang, ed., *The Wisdom of China and India* (New York: Random House, 1942), p. 62

The separation of the absolute from the relative and the treatment of the absolute as something impenetrable may be good Hinduism, but it is not the teaching of the Buddha, for whom absolute and relative were inseparable except when necessary to highlight them as aspects of a unified reality.

179

4. See Kōun Yamada, *Gateless Gate* (Los Angeles: Center Publications, 1979), p. 76.

5. Marco Pallis, *A Buddhist Spectrum* (New York: The Seabury Press, 1981), p. 10.

6. Robert Aitken, *Taking the Path of Zen* (San Francisco: North Point Press, 1982), p. 110.

7. Kōun Yamada and Robert Aitken, trans. Denkoroku, mimeo., Diamond Sangha, Honolulu & Haiku, Hawaii, Case 1.

8. William Blake, "London," *Poetry and Prose of William Blake*, ed. Geoffrey Keynes (London: Nonesuch Library, 1961), p. 75.

9. Yamada, *Gateless Gate*, p. 64.

10. See J. C. and Thomas Cleary, *The Blue Cliff Record*, 3 vols. (Boulder and London: Shambhala, 1977), III, p. 559.

11. See Edward Conze, trans., *Buddhist Wisdom Books* (London: Allen and Unwin, 1975), pp. 17–74; and D. T. Suzuki, trans., *Manual of Zen Buddhism* (New York: Grove Press, 1960), pp. 38–72.

12. See Yamada, *Gateless Gate*, p. 227.

13. Comments attributed to Bodhidharma and comments by Dogen Zenji, which appear in each of my essays on the Ten Grave Precepts were translated by Yamada Kōun Rōshi and myself from *Goi, Sanki, Sanju, Jūjūkinkai Dokugo (Soliloquy on the Five Degrees, the Three Refuges, the Three Pure Precepts, and the Ten Grave Precepts)* by Yasutani Hakuun Rōshi (Tokyo: Sanbokoryukai, 1962), pp. x–xvi; 71–97. These comments were also translated by Maezumi Taizan Rōshi in the pamphlet *Mindless Flower*, published many years ago by the Zen Center of Los Angeles and now out of print. I have used Maezumi Rōshi's work as a reference in revising the translations that Yamada Rōshi and I made originally. The comments attributed to Bodhidharma are believed by modern scholars to have been written by Hui-ssu (ancestor of the T'ien T'ai school of Buddhism) and adopted later by Zen teachers. I have retained the legend that Bodhidharma wrote them; after all Bodhidharma himself is something of a

legend. Legends fuel our practice. My reference is a personal letter from the Hui-ssu scholar Dan Stevensen dated August 22, 1983.

THE FIRST GRAVE PRECEPT
Not Killing

1. Augustus de Morgan, from Jonathan Swift; quoted from Bartlett's *Familiar Quotations* (Garden City, N.Y., 1944), p. 190.
2. See Aitken, *Taking the Path of Zen*, p. 110.
3. Ibid., p. 113.
4. William LaFleur, "Sattva: Enlightenment for Plants and Trees in Buddhism." *CoEvolution Quarterly*: (special issue) "Journal for the Protection of All Beings," No. 19, Fall 1978, pp. 47–52. Even robots have Buddha-nature; see Masahiro Mori, *The Buddha in the Robot* (Tokyo: Kyosei, 1981).

THE SECOND GRAVE PRECEPT
Not Stealing

1. "Mu" is the first koan of Zen practice. See Aitken, *Taking the Path of Zen*, Chapter Nine.
2. M. K. Gandhi, *Sarvodaya (The Welfare of All)*, ed. Bharatan Kumarappa (Ahmedabad: Navajivan, 1954), p. 12.
3. Unto Tähtinen, *Non-violence as an Ethical Principle* (Turku, Finland: Turun Yliopisto, 1964), p. 136.
4. M. K. Gandhi, *Sarvodaya*, p. 14. Cited in Tähtinen, *Non-violence as an Ethical Principle*, p. 128. Taken alone, this passage on human needs may seem anthropocentric. However, Gandhi's concern extended to the nonhuman world, as his writing on the veneration of cows makes clear. See Eric Sharp, "To Hinduism through Gandhi," *The Wisdom of the East* (Sydney: The Australian Broadcasting Commission, 1979), pp. 61–62.
5. *Letters of Rainer Maria Rilke*, 1910–1926, trans. Jan Bannard Greene and M. D. Hester Norton (New York: W. W. Norton and Co., 1969), pp. 374–375. Punctuation and

emphases are Rilke's. One of my readers remarks, "As an American, I can acknowledge the justice that is in this, but resent the generality, which seems to overstep justice. What would be more acceptable would be a judgment on the German welcome to the imported ideas."

THE THIRD GRAVE PRECEPT
Not Misusing Sex

1. Otobe Kaihō, ed., *Kosoku Zenshū Zenmon Kōan Taikan* (*A Directory of the Corpus of Ancient Zen Kōans*) (Tokyo: Kangyosha, 1974).

2. Kajitani Sōnin, ed., *Shūmon Kattōshū* (*The Traditional Tangled Wisteria Collection*) (Tokyo: Hōzōkan, 1982), pp. 342–344.

3. Otobe, *Kosoku Zenshū Zenmon Kōan Taikan*, p. 563.

4. Nyogen Senzaki, "101 Zen Stories," *Zen Flesh, Zen Bones*, Paul Reps, compiler (Rutland, Vt.: Charles E. Tuttle, 1970), p. 24.

5. Elaine Pagels, *The Gnostic Gospels* (New York: Random House, 1979), p. xv.

6. Jōshū Sasaki, *Buddha is the Center of Gravity* (San Cristobal, N.M.: Lama Foundation, 1974), p. 24.

THE FOURTH GRAVE PRECEPT
Not Lying

1. Probably a paraphrase of Dōgen Zenji's comment to the Sixth Grave Precept.

2. See Yamada, *Gateless Gate*, p. 168.

3. See Suzuki, *Manual of Zen Buddhism*, p. 98.

4. *Hamlet*, III.ii.

5. See Yamada, *Gateless Gate*, p. 125.

6. See Cleary, *The Blue Cliff Record*, I, p. 53.

7. Ibid., I, p. 54.

8. Ibid.

9. Dōgen Kigen, "*Daigo* [Great Enlightenment]." *A Complete English Translation of Dōgen Zenji's Shōbōgenzō*, trans. Kōsen Nishiyama and John Stevens, 3 vols. (Sendai: Daihokkaikaku, 1975–82), I, p. 34.

THE FIFTH GRAVE PRECEPT
Not Giving or Taking Drugs

The title reads, "Not Giving or Taking Wine" in the original Chinese. I have kept the intention, but substituted "drugs," the generic term for alcoholic beverages and other substances such as marijuana, cocaine, and Valium, which were unknown or little used when the precept was formulated.

1. Kōun Yamada and Robert Aitken, Shoyoroku, mimeo. Diamond Sangha, Honolulu & Haiku, Hawaii, Case 67.
2. See Yamada, *Gateless Gate*, p. 190.
3. Edited from D. T. Suzuki, *Essays in Zen Buddhism* (First Series) (New York: Grove Press, 1961), p. 327.
4. See Cleary, *The Blue Cliff Record*, III, p. 554.
5. Dogen Kigen, *Genjō Kōan*, trans. Hakuyu Taizan Maezumi, *The Way of Everyday Life* (Los Angeles: Center Publications, 1978), n.p.
6. Senzaki, "101 Zen Stories," *Zen Flesh, Zen Bones*, p. 43.

THE SIXTH GRAVE PRECEPT
Not Discussing Faults of Others

1. See Yamada, *Gateless Gate*, p. 13.
2. Matt. 7 : 1.
3. See Yamada, *Gateless Gate*, p. 96.
4. Aitken, *Taking the Path of Zen*, p. 110.
5. Joanna Macy, *Dharma and Development: Religion as a Resource in the Sarvodaya Self-Help Movement* (West Hartford, Conn.: Kumarian Press, 1983), pp. 60–61.
6. Benjamin Franklin, *Autobiography* (New York: Collier, 1909), p. 87.
7. Kōun Yamada, "The Stature of Yasutani Rōshi," trans. Kōun Yamada and Robert Aitken, *The Eastern Buddhist*, Vol. VII, No. 2, 1974, pp. 119–120. Commonly the Sixth Precept is interpreted as a kind of Hippocratic Oath not to mention violations of the precepts that occur within the Buddhist community when speaking with people outside the community.
8. See Cleary, *The Blue Cliff Record*, I, p. 66.

9.   Matt. 21:31.
10. See Cleary, *The Blue Cliff Record*, III, p. 614.

THE SEVENTH GRAVE PRECEPT
Not Praising Yourself While Abusing Others

1.   Philip B. Yampolsky, *The Platform Sutra of the Sixth Patriarch*
     (New York: Columbia University Press, 1967), Chinese
     text, p. 18; English text, p. 161.
2.   Ibid., Chinese text pp. 7–8; English text, p. 40.
3.   See Kōun Yamada, *Gateless Gate*, p. 72.
4.   "Torei Zenji's 'Bodhisattva's Vow,'" Daily Zen Sutras,
     mimeo. Diamond Sangha, Honolulu and Haiku, Hawaii.
5.   See Virginia Coover et al., ed., *Resource Manual for a Living
     Revolution* (Philadelphia: New Society, 1981), and The
     Training/Action Affinity Group, *Building Social Change
     Communities* (Philadelphia: Movement for a New Society,
     1979).
6.   Gary Snyder's reference was *Gotama Buddha*, by Hajime
     Nakamura (Los Angeles: Buddhist Books International,
     1977), pp. 105–106.
7.   Ibid., p. 106.
8.   Wong Mou-lam, trans., *The Sutra of Hui Neng*, Book Two of
     The Diamond Sutra and the Sutra of Hui Neng, p. 51. See Yam-
     polsky, *The Platform Sutra of the Sixth Patriarch*, p. 143 and
     note.

THE EIGHTH GRAVE PRECEPT
Not Sparing the Dharma Assets

1.   See Yamada, *Gateless Gate*, p. 19.
2.   See Suzuki, *Manual of Zen Buddhism*, p. 95.
3.   See Bernard Tetsugen Glassman, "Zen and Science: Shō-
     san," *ZCLA Journal*, Summer, 1975.
4.   Raymond B. Blackney, *Meister Eckhart: A Modern Transla-
     tion* (New York: Harper and Bros., 1941), pp. 185–186.
5.   John Blofeld, trans., *The Zen Teaching of Hui Hai on Sudden
     Illumination* (New York: Weiser, 1972), p. 52. A fascinating
     new work on gift giving, in effect the Danaparamita from

the point of view of cultural anthropology, is *The Gift: Imagination and the Erotic Life of Property*, by Lewis Hyde (New York: Random House, 1983).

6. "Kahawai Koans," trans. Thomas Cleary. *Kahawai: Journal of Women in Zen*, Winter, 1983.

7. See Francis Dojun Cook, trans., *How to Raise an Ox* (Los Angeles: Center Publications, 1978), p. 98.

8. See Yamada, *Gateless Gate*, p. 39. For a discussion of this case, see "The Nature of the Precepts."

9. Yamada and Aitken, Shoyoroku, Case 12.

10. See Masao Abe, "As Zen Comes to the West," *Blind Donkey*, Vol. 8, No. 1; Jan. 1983, p. 19.

THE NINTH GRAVE PRECEPT
Not Indulging in Anger

1. Yamada and Aitken, Shoyoroku, Case 79.

2. Aitken, *Taking the Path of Zen*, p. 110.

3. *Ts'ai Ken T'an* (*Vegetable Root Discourses*), by Hung Yingming, originally published about 1592. My translation is from the Chinese original and the Japanese translation in *Musings of a Chinese Vegetarian*, translated by Yaichiro Isobe (Tokyo: Yuhodo, 1926), p. 4. This work is also partially translated by Norman Waddell in *The Eastern Buddhist*, New Series, Vol. 2, No. 2, 1969.

4. Quoted by R. H. Blyth, *Zen in English Literature and Oriental Classics* (New York: Dutton, 1960), p. 52.

5. Harold Winfield Kent, *Dr. Hyde and Mr. Stevenson* (Rutland, Vt.: Tuttle, 1973).

6. Kōun Yamada, "The Stature of Yasutani Rōshi," p. 111.

7. Attributed to Seng Ts'an. Suzuki, *Manual of Zen Buddhism*, p. 77.

8. See Cleary, *The Blue Cliff Record*, II, p. 365.

9. Yamada, *Gateless Gate*, p. 76. The story is quoted in "The Nature of the Precepts."

10. See Suzuki, *Manual of Zen Buddhism*, p. 93.

11. My translation of the pertinent passage reads: "Dwell nowhere and bring forth that mind." See Suzuki, *Manual of*

Zen Buddhism, p. 43, and Conze, *Buddhist Wisdom Books*, pp. 47–48.

12. Thich Nhat Hanh, a talk at a Buddhist Peace Fellowship retreat, Tassajara Zen Mountain Center, March 20, 1983.

13. Blake, "A Vision of the Last Judgement," *Poetry and Prose of William Blake*, pp. 649–650.

14. C. Y. Chang, *Original Teachings of Ch'an Buddhism* (New York: Pantheon, 1969), p. 166.

THE TENTH GRAVE PRECEPT
Not Defaming the Three Treasures

1. This understanding of sangha is very different from the sectarian monastic view, which limits the term to the priesthood. Only monks and nuns who are fully ordained and have accepted the 250 precepts of ancient Buddhism (or 348 precepts in the case of nuns) and the Ten Major and the Forty-eight Minor Bodhisattva Precepts qualify for the priesthood, according to the Sino-American Buddhist Association. The minimum sangha consists of four male priests or four female priests who live together. Lay people must not assume the name "sangha" for they do not live pure lives. See "The Laity Is Not the Sangha," by Heng Chü, *Proper Dharma Seal*, Sino-American Buddhist Association, No. 1, July 4, 1983.

2. "Dedication," Daily Zen Sutras.

3. Cleary, *The Blue Cliff Record*, I, p. 37.

4. Aitken, *Taking the Path of Zen*, p. 112.

5. See "The Nature of the Precepts." "The many beings" is a translation of the Sanskrit *sattva*, literally "being, existence, entity, reality," which is translated into Chinese in at least two ways, *yu hsing* (*usei* in Japanese), meaning "having sentience" and *chung sheng* (*shujō* in Japanese), meaning "the many beings." I think we should be clear about the usage we choose. In Mahayana wisdom, all beings are sentient, including stones and clouds, so "sentient beings" as an English translation of *sattva* is either tautological, or it is a limitation to those beings that in ordinary Western wisdom we

would consider to have perception: humans, animals, and perhaps plants.

The third of the Three Pure Precepts, the first of the Four Great Vows ("Though the many beings are numberless, I vow to save them"), and sutras recited in Japanese Zen Buddhist centers all use *shujō*, "the many beings," as the translation or equivalent of *sattva*. The use of the English word "sentient" is thus not faithful to Mahayana usage or meaning, and I propose that it be dropped. Otherwise we are leaving out stones and clouds and unicorns, not to mention our feelings, which come into being and then disappear.

6. Aitken, *Taking the Path of Zen*, p. 113.
7. "Mealtime Sutras," Daily Zen Sutras.
8. See Yamada, *Gateless Gate*, p. 67.
9. Ibid., p. 158.
10. See Yoel Hoffman, *Radical Zen: The Sayings of Jōshū* (Brookline, Mass.: Autumn Press, 1978), p. 119.
11. See Yamada, *Gateless Gate*, p. 14.
12. See Hsüan Hua et al., *Flower Adornment Sutra: Pure Conduct*, Chapter 11 (Talmadge, Calif.: Buddhist Text Translation Society, 1982), p. 245.

EATING THE BLAME

1. Retold from Senzaki, "101 Zen Stories," *Zen Flesh, Zen Bones*, pp. 82–83.
2. See Cleary, *The Blue Cliff Record*, II, p. 323.
3. Ibid., III, p. 500.
4. Ibid., p. 503.
5. Yamada and Aitken, Shoyoroku, Case 21.
6. Ibid., Case 37.
7. See Hee-Jin Kim, *Dōgen Kigen: Mystical Realist* (Tucson: University of Arizona Press, 1975), pp. 78–80.

A NOTE ON SAMU

1. Giei Satō and Eshin Nishimura, *Unsui: A Diary of Monastic Life* (Honolulu: University of Hawaii, 1973), n.p. The caption reads "Working in the Garden."
2. Otobe, *Kosoku Zenshu Zenmon Kōan Taikan*, pp. 649–712.

3.   D. T. Suzuki, *The Training of the Zen Buddhist Monk* (Berkeley: Wingbow Press, 1974), pp. 33–38.

4.   Suzuki, *Essays in Zen Buddhism* (First Series), pp. 314–319.

5.   Nakamura Hajime, ed., *Bukkyōgo Daijiten*, 3 vols. (Tokyo: Tōkyō Shōseikikan, 1975), I, p. 439 (column 1).

6.   Suzuki, *Essays in Zen Buddhism* (First Series), p. 315.

7.   Yampolsky, *The Platform Sutra of the Sixth Patriarch*, Chinese text p. 2. See English text p. 128.

8.   Dogen Kigen, "Gyōji (*Principles of Practice*), Part 1," Honzanban Shukusatsu, *Shōbōgenzō* (Tokyo: Kōmeisha, 1968), p. 301.

9.   Ibid., pp. 301–302.

10. Martin Calcutt, "The Early Ch'an Monastic Rule: *Ch'ing kuei* in the Shaping of Ch'an Community Life." *Early Ch'an in China and Tibet*, ed. Whalen Lai and Lewis R. Lancaster (Berkeley: Berkeley Buddhist Studies Series, 1983), pp. 180–181.

11. Suzuki, *Essays in Zen Buddhism* (First Series), pp. 318–319.

12. Holmes Welch, *The Practice of Chinese Buddhism: 1900–1952* (Cambridge: Harvard, 1967), pp. 53–80.

13. Suzuki, *The Training of the Zen Buddhist Monk*, p. 24.

14. Ueda Mannen et al., eds., *Daijiten* (Tokyo: Kodansha, 1971), p. 1086 (column 1).

15. The Sarvodaya Movement of village self-help in Sri Lanka may be at the forefront of a shift in values in Southern Buddhism toward the Bodhisattva ideal. Joanna Macy observes that in Sarvodaya the Bodhisattva, "which historically has been more popular in Mahayāna Buddhism than in Sri Lanka, is increasingly evoked. This figure personifies action for others—a willingness to postpone enlightenment for the sake of others, rather than withdrawal from society to pursue his own release from suffering." Macy, in *Dharma and Development*, p. 75, quotes a Sarvodaya monk:

> I do not aim now for that release, or even to become a stream-winner—at least not for many lives. There is too much work to do to help my fellow beings out of poverty, greed, ignorance. I am ready to wait till everyone can enter nirvāna with me. It will take a while.

THE SELF

1. See Suzuki, *Manual of Zen Buddhism*, p. 16.
2. Ibid. In the jargon of personal liberation, "autonomy" now means "one against." This is not the Buddhist position.
3. This is the sentence D. T. Suzuki used to sum up the message of the *Diamond Sutra*. However, it cannot be found exactly in that form in the *Sutra*. See Suzuki, *Manual of Zen Buddhism*, pp. 42, 43, 49; and Conze, *Buddhist Wisdom Books*, pp. 40, 47–48, 61–62.
4. Raymond B. Blakney, trans., *Meister Eckhart: A Modern Translation* (New York: Harper & Bros., 1941), p. 3.
5. Yamada, *Gateless Gate*, p. 91.
6. Isshu Miura and Ruth Fuller Sasaki, *Zen Dust: The History of the Kōan and Kōan Study in Rinzai (Lin-chi) Zen.* (New York: Harcourt Brace and World, 1966), p. 292.
7. See Hakuyu Taizan Maezumi, *The Way of Everyday Life* (Los Angeles: Center Publications, 1978), n.p.
8. See Cleary, *The Blue Cliff Record*, III, p. 554.

THE SEARCH FOR THE MIND

1. Cleary, *The Blue Cliff Record*, II, p. 274.
2. Dom Aelred Graham, *Conversations: Christian and Buddhist* (New York: Harcourt Brace Jovanovich, 1968), p. 69. One of my friends asked, "Does the 'I don't know' mean, 'I don't know whether or not form is emptiness'? or 'I don't know what *meaning* means in relation to that statement'?" Neither one. Kobori Roshi is showing what "form is emptiness" means.
3. Cleary, *The Blue Cliff Record*, I, p. 1.
4. Blakney, *Meister Eckhart: A Modern Translation*, p. 47.
5. Thich Nhat Hanh, *The Miracle of Mindfulness: A Manual on Meditation* (Boston: Beacon Press, 1976), pp. 79 ff.
6. Yamada, *Gateless Gate*, p. 109.

BRINGING FORTH THE MIND

1. See Suzuki, *Manual of Zen Buddhism*, p. 43; and Conze, *Buddhist Wisdom Books*, pp. 47–48.

2. M. O'C. Walshe, trans., *Meister Eckhart: Sermons and Treatises*, 2 vols. (London: Watkins, 1979–1981), I, p. 2.

3. Ibid., I, p. 7.

4. Yamada and Aitken, Denkōroku, Case 51.

5. A phrase Yamada Kōun Rōshi often uses in his teaching.

6. D. T. Suzuki, *Living by Zen* (New York: Samuel Weiser, 1972), pp. 111–116.

7. Walshe, *Meister Eckhart*, I, p. 9.

8. James M. Robinson, ed., *The Nag Hammadi Library in English* (New York & London: Harper & Row, 1977), p. 121.

9. Norman Waddell, trans., "The Zen Sermons of Bankei Yōtaku, Part I"; *The Eastern Buddhist*, Vol. VII, No. 1 (1974), p. 125.

10. Kim, *Dōgen Kigen: Mystical Realist*, p. 236.

11. Kazuaki Tanahashi and Arnold Kotler, trans., "Instructions for the Tenzō (*Tenzō Kyokun*)," mimeo., Mountain Gate Study Center, Zen Center of San Francisco, 1981, p. 49; pp. 52–55.

THE MIND OF CLOVER

1. See Cleary, *The Blue Cliff Record*, I, p. 164.

2. Ibid., II, p. 424.

3. Ibid., I, p. 164.

4. See Maezumi, *The Way of Everyday Life*, n.p.

5. Dōgen Kigen: "Now I see clearly that the mind is the mountains, the rivers, and the great earth; the sun, the moon, and the stars." See Kim, *Dōgen Kigen: Mystical Realist*, p. 148.

6. One of my readers asked, "How do you reconcile all things appearing as their own reason—that is to say, independently—with the Net of Indra and universal symbiosis?" I am comfortable with this paradox. Like the identity of form and emptiness, the fact appears in nature, and it becomes a paradox only when we formulate it.

7. See Yamada, *Gateless Gate*, p. 119.

8. See, for example, Frithjof Schuon, *Gnosis: Divine Wisdom* (Bedfont, Middlesex, England: Perennial Books, 1978).

THE MORNING STAR

1. Yamada and Aitken, Shoyoroku, Case 67. See Chapter Six "Not Giving or Taking Drugs."

2. Yamada, *Gateless Gate*, pp. 13–14.

3. Aitken, "Hakuin Zenji's 'Song of Zazen,'" *Taking the Path of Zen*, p. 113.

4. George Meredith, "Lucifer in Starlight," *The Poems of George Meredith*, ed. Phyllis B. Bartlett, 2 vols. (New Haven: Yale University Press, 1978), I, p. 285.

5. See Yamada, *Gateless Gate*, p. 40.

6. See Cleary, *The Blue Cliff Record*, I, p. 1.

7. Yampolsky, *The Platform Sutra of the Sixth Patriarch*, p. 146.

8. *Basic Call to Consciousness* (Mohawk Nation, via Rooseveltown, N.Y.: Akwesasne Notes, 1978), pp. 71–72.

9. Maezumi, *The Way of Everyday Life*, n.p.

10. *Basic Call to Consciousness*, p. 11.

11. Gary Snyder, *Earth House Hold* (New York: New Directions, 1969), pp. 91–92.

12. From a poster of Chief Joseph (Mohawk Nation, via Rooseveltown, N.Y.: Akwesasne Notes, n.d.).

THE WAY AND ITS VIRTUE

1. Takashi James Kodera, *Dogen's Formative Years in China: An Historical Study and Annotated Translation of the Hōkyō-ki* (London: Routledge & Kegan Paul, 1980), pp. 23 ff.

2. 1 Cor. 13 : 13.

3. See Suzuki, *Manual of Zen Buddhism*, p. 43; and Conze, *Buddhist Wisdom Books*, pp. 47–48.

4. Aitken, *Taking the Path of Zen*, p. 110.

5. Benjamin Lynn Olson, trans., *Tao Te Ching*, unpublished ms., section 17.

RELIGIOUS ACTIVISM AND THE TAO

1. See Norman Cohn, *The Pursuit of the Millenium*, Revised and Expanded Edition (New York: Oxford University Press, 1977).

2. Alexander Jones, gen. ed., *The Jerusalem Bible* (Garden City, N.Y.: Doubleday, 1966).

3. Another interpretation: "I, the man Jesus, who am also the son of God and the true messiah, am here among you now, and this is the beginning of the end of days."

4. Joseph Campbell, *Occidental Mythology* (New York: Penguin, 1976), pp. 368–369.

5. James M. Robinson, gen. ed., *The Nag Hammadi Library* (San Francisco: Harper & Row, 1977), p. 130. Compare also, "What you look forward to has already come, but you do not recognize it," p. 123.

6. Aitken, *Taking the Path of Zen*, pp. 113.

7. Ibid., p. 112.

8. Blake, "Auguries of Innocence," *Poetry and Prose of William Blake*, p. 118.

9. Kodera, *Dogen's Formative Years in China*, pp. 23 ff.

10. Matt. 5:48.

11. Philip Kapleau, *The Three Pillars of Zen* (Boston: Beacon Press, 1967), p. 28.

12. Rom. 8:22–23.

13. Blakney, *Meister Eckhart: A Modern Translation*, pp. 79–80. See "Breakthrough: Meister Eckhart's Spirituality," in *New Translation*, ed. Mathew Fox (Garden City, N.Y.: Doubleday, 1980), p. 516.

14. See Yamada, *Gateless Gate*, p. 14.

15. Blake, "Milton," *Poetry and Prose of William Blake*, p. 376.

GANDHI, DŌGEN, AND DEEP ECOLOGY

Thanks to George Sessions, whose paper, "Spinoza, Perennial Philosophy, and Deep Ecology," was a direct inspiration for this essay. (Mimeo., Sierra College, Rocklin, Calif., 1979). I am told that Arne Naess, the Norwegian eco-philosopher who coined the term, "deep ecology," is now using the expression, "New Philosophy of Nature," as something less divisive and invidious.

1. Jag Parvesh Chander, *Teachings of Mahatma Gandhi* (Lahore: The India Book Works, 1945), p. 375. (Tähtinen, *Non-violence as an Ethical Principle*, p. 83.)

2. Thomas Merton, *Gandhi on Non-violence* (New York: New Directions, 1965), p. 5.

3. See Maezumi, *The Way of Everyday Life*, n.p.
4. Blake, "Auguries of Innocence," *Poetry and Prose of William Blake*, p. 118.
5. Genesis 9:2.
6. William Wordsworth, "Expostulation and Reply," *Lyrical Ballads*, ed. W. J. B. Owens (New York, etc.: Oxford University Press, 1967), p. 104.
7. Sessions, "Spinoza, Perennial Philosophy, and Deep Ecology," p. 15. Space is too limited for a complete discussion of deep ecology, which naturally must include provision for agriculture and other kinds of environmental management. It is the mind-set that would exploit the future and exterminate species that the ecophilosophers wish to see turned around.
8. Erik H. Erikson, *Gandhi's Truth: On the Origins of Militant Nonviolence* (New York: Norton, 1969), especially p. 251.
9. Matt. 25:40.

Glossary

Abhidharma—(Sanskrit) Treatise Commentary; one of the main parts of Buddhist literature

anuttara samyak sambodhi—(Sanskrit) perfect, all-penetrating enlightenment

Avalokiteśvara—(Sanskrit) "One who perceives the self at rest," or "One who hears the sounds of the world;" the incarnation of mercy and compassion; *see Kanjizai and Kanzeon*

bodhimanda—(Sanskrit) spot or place of enlightenment of the Buddha under the Bodhi tree; *see dōjō*

bodhi tree—bo or pipal tree (*ficus religiosa*); *see bodhimanda and dōjō*

bodhisattva—(Sanskrit) one on the path to enlightenment; one who is enlightened; one who enlightens others; ideal of Northern Buddhism

Buddha—(Sanskrit) enlightened one; Śākyamuni; one of several figures in the Buddhist pantheon; a being

Burakumin—(Japanese) the outcast class, formerly confined to specific neighborhoods or villages, and to certain occupations

Ch'an-shih—(Chinese) Zenji; Zen master (an honorific title)

Coordinating Group for Religion in Society—an international movement for self-development among oppressed people, centered in Thailand, founded by Sulak Sivaraksa

dāna—(Sanskrit) charity

195

Dānapāramitā—(Sanskrit) the Perfection of Charity

Dhammapada—(Pali) *Path of Virtue*; a Theravāda collection of didactic verses

Dharma—(Sanskrit) law: religious, secular, natural; the Law of Karma; affinity, phenomena; Tao or Way; a teaching; the void

Dharmakāya—(Sanskrit) Law Body (of the Buddha); the pure, clear, empty aspect of the universe

dhyāna—(Sanskrit) absorption; the form of meditation; *see samādhi*

Dhyānapāramitā—(Sanskrit) the Perfection of Meditation

Diamond Sūtra— *Vajracchedikā Sūtra*; one of the central texts of the *Prajñāpāramitā* literature

dōjō—(Japanese) the Zen training center; one's own place of enlightenment; *see bodhimanda*

dokusan—(Japanese) sanzen; to go or work alone; personal interview with the rōshi

Eightfold Path—the basic outline of Buddhist practice; upright views, thinking, speech, action, livelihood, effort, mindfulness, and meditation

gasshō—(Japanese) añjali; hands palm to palm in a spirit of respect or devotion

gāthā—(Sanskrit) verse in praise of the Buddha or as a succinct restatement of Buddhist truth

go—(Japanese) a board game played with black and white stones

Harada-Yasutani line—the Japanese Sōtō Zen Buddhist school founded by the twentieth century teachers, Harada Dai'un and Yasutani Haku'un

Harijan—(Sanskrit) Children of God; Gandhi's term for the Panchama, the "untouchable" class of India

Heart Sūtra—a condensation of the *Prajñāpāramitā* literature

Hīnayāna—(Sanskrit) Lesser Vehicle, a Northern Buddhist term for the Southern Buddhism of Sri Lanka, Burma, and Southeast Asia

Hua-yen Sūtra—the last great compendium of Mahāyāna literature, completed in China in the eighth century, derived from the Sanskrit *Avatamsaka Sūtra*

Ittōen—(Japanese) Garden of One Light; community service and crafts movement founded by Nishida Tenkō

Kanjizai—(Japanese) Avalokitesvara; The One Who Perceives the [Essential] Self at Rest; the one who perceives the emptiness of perceptions and forms; *see Kanzeon*

Kannon—(Japanese) Kanzeon

Kanzeon—(Japanese) Avalokitesvara; The One Who Perceives the Sounds of the World; incarnation of mercy and compassion; *see Kanjizai*

karma—(Sanskrit) action; cause and effect; affinity; the world of cause and effect or affinity

"Katsu!"—(Japanese) "Hō!" the shout given by Zen masters that wipes away everything

kenshō—(Japanese) to see nature; to see into essential nature; gnostic experience in Zen practice

kinhin—(Japanese) sūtra walk; the formal group walk between periods of zazen

kōan—(Japanese) relative/absolute; an expression of harmony of empty oneness with the world of particulars; a theme of zazen to be made clear

Mādhyamika—(Sanskrit) The Middle View, expounding the main doctrines of the *Prajñāpāramitā* literature

Mahāyāna—(Sanskrit) Great Vehicle; the Northern Buddhism of China, Korea, and Japan (Vajrayāna, or Tibetan Buddhism is often included in this classification)

Maitreya—(Sanskrit) Friendly; Benevolent; the Buddha of the future

mani—(Sanskrit) talisman; pearl; symbol of the Buddha and of Buddhist wisdom

Māra—(Sanskrit) The Destroyer; an influence of vicious ignorance

Middle Way—the Mahāyāna resolution of form and emptiness, or of karma and essential nature

mind—depending on context: the human brain, heart, or spirit; or the nature of the universe and its phenomena

mochi—(Japanese) rice cake

mondō—(Japanese) question and answer; Zen dialogue, usually between teacher and student

Mt. Gṛdhrakūṭa—Vulture Peak in Patna, India, where the Buddha preached

Mu—(Japanese) Wu; No; does not have; case one of the *Wu-men kuan*, often the first kōan of the Zen student

nen—(Japanese) thought; one thought frame

Net of Indra—in Hua-yen thought, the multidimensional net of phenomena in which each point or knot is a jewel that perfectly reflects all other points

nirvana (nirvāna)—(Sanskrit) extinction of craving; the wisdom presented in the world of particulars

pāramitā—(Sanskrit) perfection, Buddhahood

parinirvāna—(Sanskrit) ultimate nirvana; death

Platform Sūtra—sayings and doings of Hui-neng, eighth century

Prajñāpāramitā—(Sanskrit) Perfection of Wisdom; Buddhahood; the formative teaching of Mahāyāna

right livelihood—one step of the Eightfold Path

Rinzai—(Japanese) the Rinzai Zen Buddhist Sect, traced from Lin-chi, ninth century

rōshi—(Japanese) venerable teacher

saké—(Japanese) rice wine

samādhi—(Sanskrit) concentration; the quality of meditation; *see dhyāna*

Sambhogakāya—(Sanskrit) Body of Enjoyment; the "full and complete" body of the Buddha

samsāra—(Sanskrit) flow; transmigration; the transitory world of phenomena

samu—(Japanese) work service (in the sense of sūtra service); meditation in work (traditionally in and about the temple)

sangha (samgha)—(Sanskrit) aggregate; Buddhist priesthood; Buddhist fellowship; fellowship; harmony of Buddha and Dharma

Sarvodaya Shramadana—(Sanskrit) Awakening of All; a village self-help movement in Sri Lanka founded by A. T. Ariyaratna

satyagraha—(Sanskrit) Holding the Truth; the power of non-violent action

School of Youth for Social Service—a youth corps founded in Vietnam during the civil war by Thich Nhat Hanh

self—depending on context: Buddha; the human individual; phenomena that are experienced by the individual sesshin—(Japanese) to touch, receive, or convey the mind; the Zen retreat, conventionally seven days

skandhas—(Sanskrit) perceptions and what they perceive; forms, sensation, thought, conceptual power, and consciousness

Sōtō—(Japanese) The Sōtō Zen Buddhist Sect, traced from Tung-shan Liang-chieh, ninth century

takuhatsu—(Japanese) to show the bowl; to show the way of the Buddha; the walk taken by monks or nuns through towns near the temple to accept money or rice as contributions

tantra—(Sanskrit) A pan-Indian religious form involving magical ritual, dependence on a guru, and sometimes sexual practices

Tao—(Chinese) Bodhi or enlightenment; Way; the way of, or to enlightenment

Tathāgata—(Sanskrit) Thus Come (or Go); one who thus (or just) comes; Buddha

te—(Chinese) toku

teishō—(Japanese) presentation of the call; the rōshi's Dharma talk

Theravāda—(Pali) Way of the Elders; modern Buddhism in South and Southeast Asia

toku—(Japanese) te; power or virtue; strength of character arising from virtue and service

upāya—(Sanskrit) skillful means; compassion

Vajrayāna—(Sanskrit) Diamond Way; Tibetan Buddhism

Vārāṇasī—(Sanskrit) modern Banaras, where the Buddha first preached

zafu—(Japanese) the cushion used for zazen

zazen—(Japanese) seated meditation; dhyāna; Zen meditation

Zen—(Japanese) Ch'an; the Zen Buddhist sect; the harmony of empty oneness and the world of particulars

Zenji—(Japanese) Ch'an-shih; Zen master (an honorific title)

ABOUT THE AUTHOR

Robert Aitken's introduction to Zen came in a Japanese prison camp during World War II, after he was captured as a civilian in Guam. R. H. Blyth, author of *Zen in English Literature*, was imprisoned in the same camp, and in this unlikely setting Aitken began the first of several important apprenticeships. After the war Aitken Roshi returned often to Japan to study. He became friends with D.T. Suzuki, and studied with Nagakawa Soen Roshi and Yasutani Hakuun Roshi.

In 1959 Robert Aitken and his wife, Anne, established a Zen organization, the Diamond Sangha, which has two zendos in Hawaii. Aitken was given the title "Roshi" and authorized to teach by Yamada Koun Roshi, his current teacher, in 1974. He continues to teach and study Zen in Hawaii, where he has lived since the age of five.